A BODY BROKEN FOR A BROKEN PEOPLE

EUCHARIST IN THE
NEW TESTAMENT

FRANCIS J MOLONEY, SDB

D1113929

COLLINS DOVE
Melbourne Australia

In Gratitude for
the Long and Eucharistic life
of my Father: Denis Patrick Moloney

Published by Collins Dove
25–37 Huntingdale Road
Burwood, Victoria 3125

© Copyright Francis J. Moloney 1990
All rights reserved. Except as provided by Australian copyright law,
no part of this book may be reproduced without permission
in writing from the publishers.

First published 1990
Designed by Sarn Potter
Cover design by Sarn Potter
Cover illustration by Andrew Wichlinski

Typeset in Australia by Bookset, North Melbourne
Printed in Australia by Griffin Press Limited

The National Library of Australia
Cataloguing-in-Publication Data:

Moloney, Francis J.
  A body broken for a broken people.
  Bibliography.
  Includes index.
  ISBN 0 85924 892 5.
  1. Bible. N.T. Gospels — Criticism, interpretation,
  etc. 2. Lord's Supper — Biblical teaching.
  3. Lord's Supper — Catholic Church. I. Title

232.957

FOREWORD

In reading these pages I have heard the sound of the Good News. Wonderful, but infrequently heard. Jesus lived the Gospel of mercy, and he proclaimed it without faltering. What is more, he spoke first of all to the poor, the broken. In Jesus' vision of things, what matters is not righteousness in the observance of the commandments, but unconditional commitment to his person, love of God and love of others. Applied to the contemporary celebration of the eucharistic liturgy, is this preferential love of Jesus still visible? Has Jesus' call to joy been stifled by the detailed indications concerning who might or might not participate in the mystery? Has the Good News been carefully stored away in silos, in an attempt to preserve it better? So that it may never be deprived of its youth, it needs to be let loose into the open air. Frank Moloney guides us to listen carefully to the ever-clear voice of a Living Word.

He has approached the difficult problem of the authentic Gospel message over against a tendency to restrict eucharistic practice to a closed circle of 'the pure'. This is an ancient tendency. Paul himself gave rules of discernment for access to the sacred mysteries. It was a concern of the second and third century Church, which did not feel able to hold to its bosom certain 'sinners', such as those who had fallen away into apostasy. This self-defensive reflex action of the institutionalised body of the Church ought, nevertheless, to be always counterbalanced by a profound reflection upon the attitude of Jesus of Nazareth. Here, beside many others, the exegete exercises his office in the Church; he must, in season and out of season, assist ecclesial practice ceaselessly to renew itself.

Will one ever be able to say the last word on this question? Such a hope appears somewhat naïve to me, both from the side of the institutionalised Church and from the side of the exegetes. Thus my opinion differs from that of the author on some minor issues: I do not think that Matthew depended directly upon Mark, nor do I accept his structure of John 13, nor his suggestion that the morsel of bread offered by Jesus to Judas was eucharistic. But the essential point lies, not in certain exegetical presuppositions, but in one clearly given fact: the institution of the Eucharist is always linked to a mention of Judas the traitor and the prophecy of the denials and failure of the disciples. All exegetes agree on that point.

Frank Moloney has pushed this evidence one step further, suggesting that the Eucharist was understood by the early Church as instituted for the broken. This is a stimulating hypothesis, which deserves consideration.

I rejoice to see an exegete taking a courageous look at a pastoral problem. He has performed a task too often abandoned by the specialist who imagines that he has completed his work when he thinks that he has determined the meaning of the texts. He should do more. He should always be concerned with the pastoral impact of his affirmations, particularly when explaining the contexts within which the most important actions of Jesus of Nazareth took place. Indeed, we have become accustomed to speaking of the institution of the Eucharist without taking into account the existential context within which this institution took place.

It is here that we have a tendency to simplify the data. Which one of us is able to regard himself or herself as 'worthy' to approach the Eucharist? Do I practise all the demands of the Sermon on the Mount? It is thus that I approach the Table of the Lord with a contrite heart. Yes, the Eucharist is there for the broken. This book, which I am introducing to you, shows that clearly. One question remains. What are we to think of the situation of that person who clearly offends the present law of the Church and who is unable, for all sorts of reasons, to renounce that situation judged by the Church, quite rightly, as irregular? Has the Church the right to ban these broken people from eucharistic practice?

The answer to this difficult question cannot come from a purely exegetical study. Only the consensus of the Church can correctly appreciate its interior resistence to the poison that unlimited eucharistic access of one or other member whom it considers 'guilty' may generate. But exegetical endeavour is indispensable to prevent the Church from resting sleepily on past practices. The critical function of those who have been entrusted by the Church to spell out the immediate meaning of the biblical texts must go on without ceasing.

Ecclesial behaviour is determined by two factors:
1. the Church's place in each epoch;
2. its need to be critical of that epoch.

Who does not go forward falls back, as the ancient Fathers of the Desert used to say. However, in order to go forward it is necessary to lose momentarily the balance one had in the previously acquired situation. It is necessary to keep putting one's foot forward, and in this way eventually regain the balance that had been briefly lost.

Frank Moloney invites us not to settle for acquired positions of strength. They must always be challenged with the demands of the Gospel message.

Xavier Léon-Dufour
Paris (Centre Sèvres)

AUTHOR'S NOTE

Unless otherwise stated, Scripture quotations are taken from the Revised Standard Version of the Bible, copyright 1952 and 1971 by the division of Christian Education of the National Council of the Churches of Christ in the USA. On a few occasions the author provides his own translation. This will be indicated. Quotations from the Second Vatican Council are taken from A. Flannery (ed.), *Vatican Council II: The Conciliar and Post Conciliar Documents* (Dublin: Dominican Publications, 1975).

ACKNOWLEDGEMENTS

I am dedicating this book to my ninety-year-old father, now suffering severely from Alzheimer's disease. In his present brokenness his gentleness and genuine concern for others is still clear. As his whole life has been eucharistic, so now his final sickness proclaims the Lord's death until he comes. He would have never reached his ninetieth birthday (or his ninety-first year, as he loved to say) if it had not been for the love and commitment of my mother and the dedication and care of the Little Sisters of the Poor at Northcote.

I would like to record my thanks to a group of fellow scholars and friends who read part or the whole of my work: Brendan Byrne, SJ, Mark Coleridge, Peter Cross, Rod Doyle, CFC, Michael FitzPatrick, OFM, John Prest, SDB and Nerina Zanardo, FSP. I am particularly grateful for the lively interest that Xavier Léon-Dufour, SJ, took in it, despite his many other serious obligations. David Lovell, then Editorial Director of Collins Dove, originally proposed this book to me. It exists because of his interest. Although I am responsible for all that follows, these people have also shown me that the Eucharist is not only cult; it is life.

Francis J. Moloney, SDB
St Margaret Mary's Parish
North Brunswick, Vic. 3056
5 June 1989

CONTENTS

LIST OF ABBREVIATIONS

I have given complete titles for journals and series within the text. On a few occasions I have used the following recognised abbreviations.

AA.VV   Various Authors.

BCE   Before the Common Era.

CD   The Damascus Document (Qumran).

CE   Common Era.

JB   The Jerusalem Bible.

JSOT   Journal for the Study of the Old Testament.

NT   New Testament.

OT   Old Testament.

PL   *Patrologiae cursus completus, series latina* (ed. J. P. Migne).

1QS   The Community Rule (Qumran).

RSV   Revised Standard Version (of the Bible).

SBL   Society for Biblical Literature.

SCM   Students' Christian Movement.

SNTS   Societas Novi Testamenti Studiorum.

SPCK   Society for the Propogation of Christian Knowledge.

WUNT   Wissenschaftliche Untersuchungen zum Neuen Testament.

Introduction

'The Lord Jesus on the night when he was betrayed took bread, and when he had given thanks, he broke it, and said, "This is my body, broken for you. Do this in remembrance of me ... This cup is the new covenant in my blood. Do this ... in remembrance of me." For as often as you eat this bread and drink this cup, you proclaim the Lord's death until he comes' (see 1 Cor. 11:24–26).[1] Paul has called his erring Corinthian converts to task by telling them the story of Jesus' words and actions 'on the night when he was betrayed' (v. 23).

That same story has been told and retold for almost two thousand years. Christians have told the eucharistic story, enshrined within the liturgy, in the Church's response to the command of Jesus: 'Do this in memory of me' (Luke 22:19; 1 Cor. 11:24, 25).

---

[1] The words 'broken for you' over the bread may not be original, even though widely attested in early manuscripts. I am using it as it speaks directly to the argument of this book. For detail, see B. M. Metzger, *A Textual Commentary on the Greek New Testament* (London/New York: United Bible Societies, 1971) p. 562. Against Metzger, and defending the text as cited, see J. Duplacy, 'A propos d'un lieu variant de 1 Co 11, 24: "Voici mon corps (—, rompu, donné etc.) pour vous" ', in AA.VV, *Le Corps et le corps du Christ dans la Première Epître aux Corinthiens* (Lectio Divina 114; Paris: Cerf, 1983) 27–46.

However, this story has not only been told in the liturgy. It has been told just as significantly in the lives of Christians who have been prepared to break their own bodies and spill their own blood in a deeply eucharistic way, proclaiming 'the Lord's death until he comes' (1 Cor. 11:26).

Rooted in the broken body and the spilt blood of Jesus himself, the Eucharist has always been the story of a body broken for a broken people. This is the aspect of the central mystery of the Christian life that I would like to highlight through the New Testament study that follows. Above all, I wish to show that the Eucharist is the celebrated and lived expression of a love so great that we have never been able to match it.

Such love, however, raises some difficult questions to its institutionalisation. As a twenty-first century Church looks back upon its history, it must honestly and critically ask whether or not it has lost touch with its founding story. I wish to pose some questions that arise from a contemporary reading of that story.

This study has been a long time in the making. Through my years of teaching the New Testament I have been increasingly surprised by an overwhelming impression that the eucharistic passages in the New Testament proclaim the presence of the love of God, made visible in Jesus, to a broken people. I began to articulate this impression in various lectures from 1986–88. I eventually published some preliminary results of my research into this question in a scholarly article.[2]

What follows reaches beyond the limitations that I imposed upon myself for that more scholarly study. It is an attempt to speak to as many people as possible so that they may more deeply appreciate both the beauty and the risk of celebrating Eucharist. Scholarly articles in journals reach only small circles of subscribers. A book has a chance of reaching a wider public.

I look first at the place of a biblical study of the New Testament material that questions a well-established tradition in the Christian Churches (Chapter One). The next chapter (Chapter Two) will be dedicated to Mark 6:31–44 and 8:1–10 (the feeding miracles) and with Mark 14:17–31 (the Last Supper). My concern will be to rediscover what Mark was attempting to say to his community about its celebration of the Eucharist through his telling of the story of Jesus. I will set each single eucharistic text within the wider context of the narrative flow of the Gospel story. I presuppose that we can best find what Mark (or Matthew, Luke or John) is telling his readers or listeners by looking at the whole story, not merely the

---

[2] F. J. Moloney, 'The Eucharist as the Presence of Jesus to the Broken', *Pacifica* 2 (1989) 151–74.

part that appears most immediately relevant to our search for eucharistic thought and practice.

Although at first sight very similar, there is need to study Matthew's re-telling of the same stories: Matthew 14:13–21 and 15:32–39 (the feeding miracles) and 26:20–35 (the Last Supper). Matthew's account is not an unreflected copying of his source, Mark.[3] Attention must be given to Matthew's pastoral concern for his particular community through his well-considered use of these accounts (Chapter Three). Again we must look more widely than the passages themselves, into their narrative contexts.

Chapter Four will be devoted entirely to the Lucan material: Luke 9:10–17 (the feeding miracle), 22:14–38 (the Supper) and 24:13–35 (Emmaus) read in close association with the final meal with the eleven apostles (24:36–49). This list itself indicates that Luke has his own way of telling the story of Jesus. He has only one feeding miracle, while Mark and Matthew both have two. He also adds the story of the walk to Emmaus. This significant narrative is found nowhere else in the New Testament.[4] Luke's ability to 'tell a good story' is reflected in his very personal use of the more traditional material of the feeding miracle and the last supper.[5] Careful attention to Luke's way of telling his story will help us discover his particular point of view.

In his story of Jesus' last encounter with his disciples the Fourth Evangelist gives no explicit account of a meal tradition that contains words of institution. Although scholars often dismiss this Evangelist's contribution to eucharistic theology,[6] the important eucharistic teachings in John 6:51c–58 and 19:34 must not be ignored. Through a detailed study of John 13:1–38 (Chapter Five) I shall suggest that, while the Eucharist is not at the centre of the narrative found in the

---

[3] I presuppose that Matthew and Luke both used Mark and a further common source, usually called 'Q' (from the German word *Quelle* = source). I am aware that this presupposition is nowadays questioned. I would largely adhere to the case argued by J. A. Fitzmyer, 'The Priority of Mark and the "Q" Source in Luke', in *To Advance the Gospel: New Testament Studies* (New York: Crossroad, 1981) pp. 3–40. Neither Mark, Matthew nor Luke, however, can be understood in terms of their 'sources'. They grew within a context of a living tradition that will never be subject to scholarly control.

[4] There is, of course, a hint of it in the 'longer ending' of Mark (Mark 16:12–13). This passage does not belong to Mark's Gospel, but to a later scribe. See below, p. 21, note 9.

[5] The originality of Luke's Gospel is a fine example of that 'living tradition' mentioned above, in note 3.

[6] See, for example, R. Kysar, *The Fourth Evangelist and His Gospel: An Examination of Contemporary Scholarship* (Minneapolis: Augsburg, 1975) pp. 249–59. He concludes his (excellent) survey of current scholarship: 'The fourth gospel represents a maverick form of Christianity, to be sure, in which the sacraments, at first at least, were not known or practiced' (p. 259) [American spelling].

first section of the Gospel's Last Discourse, there is much to learn from John's use of Jesus' gift of the morsel on the night he was betrayed.

My final study of a New Testament passage (Chapter Six) will focus most of its attention on 1 Corinthians 11:17–34, a passage that has long been used to distance so-called sinners from the eucharistic table. Especially important over the centuries, for this end, has been 11:27: 'Whoever, therefore, eats the bread or drinks the cup of the Lord in an unworthy manner will be guilty of profaning the body and blood of the Lord.' However, as always in a study of the Pauline literature, we must attempt to rediscover the precise situation in the Corinthian Church that led Paul to quote from his tradition of the eucharistic words of Jesus himself (see vv. 23–25) in his debate with his converts. This rediscovery will lead us to a consideration of 1 Corinthians 10:14–22 and its wider context. The practice of the blessing of the cup and the breaking of the bread is used to exhort the Corinthians to a more committed Christian form of life in a pagan world.

Only on the basis of the data that I hope to assemble from the inspired pages of the New Testament itself do I have any right to raise some final questions. Is it possible that the early Church's understanding and practice of sharing the eucharistic table originated in its own experience of meals shared with Jesus? How does the practice of Jesus' table-fellowship relate to the Church's celebration of the Eucharist? At the Second Vatican Council, the Church described herself as 'clasping sinners to her bosom, at once holy and always in need of purification' (*Lumen Gentium* 8). In the light of the practice of Jesus' own table and the eucharistic practice of the early Church revealed to us in the authoritative Word of God in the scriptures, is our contemporary Church still 'clasping sinners to her bosom'?

Many pastoral and theological arguments could and should be raised both for and against the issues addressed here. Thus, although I am mainly interested in the questions that the Word of God raises, my concluding chapter (Chapter Seven) will also furnish some final theological reflections and more practical considerations that flow from my analysis of the New Testament texts.

This is not only a book for scholars, even though the footnotes will refer to contemporary scholarship. I have attempted to write it in a way that would be accessible to all people interested in the celebration and living of the Eucharist in the Christian Churches.

CHAPTER ONE

Raising questions

*I*t can be said, without too much fear of error, that each major period of the history of the Church's life has been marked by its own particular eucharistic theology and practice.[1] Many factors have led to the predominant understanding and practice of Eucharist in the tradition to which each of us belongs. While some of these factors are inevitably cultural and thus historically conditioned, the story of Jesus' celebration of the final meal with his disciples has always guided the eucharistic thought and practice of the Christian Churches.

In the light of the New Testament, I would like to ask an important and delicate question. Who should be admitted to the reception of the eucharistic species at the celebration of the Eucharist? It is a question that has touched all the Christian Churches, all of whom celebrate the Lord's Supper. One of the principles used in the administration of the Eucharist in all the Christian Churches is that we can permit this encounter with the Lord only to those whom, as far as we can judge, are worthy of such intimacy. There may be

---

[1] For a study of the historical development of the theology and celebration of the Eucharist, see L. Bouyer, *Eucharist: Theology and Spirituality of the Eucharistic Prayer* (Notre Dame: University of Notre Dame Press, 1968). For a briefer survey see J. H. Emminghaus, *The Eucharist: Essence, Form, Celebration* (Collegeville: Liturgical Press, 1978) pp. 39–98.

many differences in the way in which the various Christian Churches celebrate Eucharist. Yet, however far apart we may be in the cultural expression of our eucharistic faith, we are at one in our practice of 'excluding' certain people from the Table of the Lord: the Eucharist is not for sinners.

The Eucharist: not for Sinners?

The practice of excluding certain people from full participation in the celebration of the Eucharist has long been a part of the sacramental discipline of the Christian Churches. As we will see in the final chapter of this book, the Christian Churches have an important duty and responsibility to exercise such discipline.[2] The Roman Catholic Church has codified this discipline in the official book of the Church's legislation, the *Code of Canon Law*.

This so-called 'Code' (Latin *Corpus*) has a long history, originating in the practice of the earliest ecumenical councils, which settled matters of uncertainty and dispute by solemn pronouncements on questions of doctrine and discipline. Over the centuries other authoritative pronouncements were made and accepted by the Church catholic. A decisive stage was reached about 1140 when Gratian issued his *Decretum*, which collected the 'canons'. A variety of other collections led to the eventual post-Tridentine promulgation of a single printed 'corpus' in general use after 1580. This was thoroughly revised and promulgated for the Catholic Church in 1917.[3] The Second Vatican Council asked for a further revision (see *Christus Dominus* 44; *Apostolicam actuositatem* 1; *Ad Gentes* 14), which was promulgated in its revised form as recently as 25 January 1983.

The Canons dealing with the admission of people to the eucharistic table read as follows:

> Those who are excommunicated or interdicted after the imposition or declaration of the penalty and others who obstinately persist in manifest grave sin are not to be admitted to Holy Communion. (Canon 915)
> A person who is conscious of grave sin is not to celebrate Mass or to receive the body of the Lord without prior sacramental confession unless a grave reason is present and there is no opportunity of confessing; in this case the person is to be mindful of the obligation to make an act of perfect contrition,

---

[2] See below, pp. 131–4.

[3] For a concise historical survey, with further bibliography, see the articles 'Canon Law' and 'Corpus Iuris Canonici' in F. L. Cross & E. A. Livingstone (eds), *The Oxford Dictionary of the Christian Church* (Oxford: Oxford University Press, 1974), 2nd ed., pp. 231 and 349.

including the intention of confessing as soon as possible. (Canon 916)[4]

The Second Vatican Council speaks of the importance of the regular and total participation of the faithful in the celebration of the Eucharist (see especially *Sacrosanctum Concilium* 48, 55), but offers no suggestions on the discipline of 'exclusion' from full participation. Thus it was left to the legislative arm of the Church to look to these important questions.

In practice, this legislation, with its long standing in Christian tradition, leads to the reception of the Eucharist officially being denied to an increasing number of Catholics. Faced with the complexity of modern secular society, there are now many Catholics whose marriages are not in accord with official teaching.[5] There is also a growing number of good people struggling with the Catholic Church's teaching on birth control. Although this latter issue is a more 'private concern', such people often have difficulties in approaching the eucharistic table out of their loyalty to the Catholic Church and its teaching.

One could add to this the issue of intercommunion with non-Catholic Christians.[6] Our present legislation hinges upon someone's being considered not fully prepared for the reception of the eucharistic Lord in our tradition.[7] I have mentioned some issues, but there are many other difficult situations, better known to the individuals themselves and their pastors, which could be added to this list of well-known difficulties.

Such a disciplinary practice reflects a eucharistic theology that has its own history and tradition in the Western Church. Does anyone have a right to question it? May one compare this important

---

[4] The translation of the Canons is taken from Canon Law Society of America, *Code of Canon Law: Latin-English Edition* (Washington: Canon Law Society of America, 1983) p. 343.

[5] For the subsequent discussion of this issue, especially at the 1980 synod on the family and the subsequent Apostolic Exhortation *Familiaris Consortio* (22 November 1981), see J. M. Huels, *One Table, Many Laws: Essays on Catholic Eucharistic Practice* (Collegeville: Liturgical Press, 1986) pp. 74–84.

[6] The present position of the Catholic Church is described in Huels, *One Table*, pp. 85–97.

[7] I am well aware that there is much more to the ecumenical question, especially as regards ecclesiology, and the theology of ministry, particularly the latter. An uncritical and indiscriminate 'intercommunion' without regard for one's theology of ministry can lead to serious ecumenical problems. For that reason I chose the expression 'not fully prepared', as its vagueness can cover a multitude of difficulties. On this, see Mark Brolly's report on my recent intervention on this issue in 'Theologian sees potential harm in intercommunion', *Age*, Monday, 6 February 1989, p. 13.

tradition enshrined in the official legislation of the Church to the various other cultural and historical issues that were examined by the great renewal process set in motion by the Second Vatican Council? May one raise the question of the 'Christianity' of the practice of excluding the broken people, those we judge as sinners, from the eucharistic table?

While never denying its crucial importance for the life of the Church, one must not divinise legislation. There are certainly laws that are 'written on our hearts' (see Rom. 2:14), but most of our laws are also the results of history and culture. Most people today are aware that there are laws in both the Church and society that are more oppressive than creative. The very existence of an official body for the ongoing interpretation of the new Code of Canon Law is an indication of the Church's awareness of this fact.[8]

Despite the existence of such 'official' bodies, there is nowadays a widespread grass-roots feeling that our current traditions concerning the admission of people to the eucharistic table need to be questioned and possibly re-thought. More than one pastor has told me that he is acting on the basis of his own pastoral sense. This means that, at the level of practice, people traditionally excluded from the Eucharist are now simply admitted, without further ado.[9] However, it is methodologically unsound to go ahead, either theologically or pastorally, on the basis of 'a widespread grass-roots feeling'.[10]

Many of the important renewing movements in the history of the Church often appear to have come from this practice, but it is not sufficient in itself. Such pastoral practice is based on one's 'feeling' about the issue. No matter how finely tuned a particular pastor may be to the ways of the Spirit in the Church, the biblical and theological motivations for or against such practice must be considered. The Catholic tradition cannot be renewed only on the

---

[8] The Pontifical Commission for the Interpretation of Canon Law, at present (1989) under the Presidency of Cardinal Rosalio J. Castillo Lara.

[9] See M. Barth, *Rediscovering the Lord's Supper: Communion with Israel, with Christ, and Among the Guests* (Atlanta: John Knox Press, 1988) p. 2: 'It is a public scandal that many Christian communities exploit the doctrine and the celebration of the communion as a means of excommunication. This scandal persists, even though brave and risky steps are taken by pastors and priests, by student groups and scholars, by deacons and so-called laypeople, to redress this situation in several countries, especially in the framework of local congregations.' Barth's provocative book, playing down all concept of real presence, or ministerial priesthood and high sacramentality, is one-sided, but makes some excellent exegetical and pastoral points.

[10] I am aware that some pastors work on the principle of 'internal forum' in the question of admitting the divorced to the Eucharist, in the light of a letter of Cardinal Seper (11 April 1973). For a careful, approving study of this approach, see Huels, *One Table*, pp. 74–84.

basis of practice. Its claims to be a 'revealed religion' are central to its very being. As such, the pastoral — as well as the spiritual — 'renewal' of the Catholic tradition must also have its roots in a continual reflection on the richness of the Word of God in the Bible and the great Traditions of the Church. It is in the light of these factors that the Magisterium, adopting an attitude of listening and learning, should eventually teach.

A Return to the Original Design

Pope Paul VI once wrote of his understanding of his particular role in the process of working to make the Church what it was founded to be:

> We should always wish to lead her [the Church] back to her perfect form corresponding, on the one hand to her original design and, on the other, fully consistent with the necessary development which, like a seed grown into a tree, has given to the Church her legitimate and concrete form in history. (*Ecclesiam Suam* 83)[11]

It is important, therefore, that we search for a more solid basis upon which to position our feet, if we wish to raise a questioning finger to a tradition that has found its way into the Church's official legislation. We too have a responsibility to search out the Church's 'original design'. Any suggestion that the authentic Christian tradition has in some way been 'distorted' over the centuries must reach back to a period and a situation before those distortions. As Rosemary Ruether has so clearly indicated:

> To look back to some original base of meaning and truth before corruption is to know that truth is more basic than falsehood . . . One cannot wield the lever of criticism without a place to stand.[12]

This 'original base of meaning' concerns me throughout this study. My attention was first drawn to the issue because of the pastoral concerns that I have just mentioned. However, the question at stake, the 'original base of meaning', is much deeper than the pastoral questions, important as they may be.

It is often taken for granted that the Eucharist is celebrated by a holy Church for a holy people. Precisely because of this presupposition the exclusion of the sinful from such celebrations must follow

---

[11] *Encyclical Letter Ecclesiam Suam with a Discussion Aid Outline* (Homebush: St Paul Publications, 1964) p. 25.

[12] R. Ruether, *Sexism and God-Talk: Towards a Feminist Theology* (London: SCM Press, 1983) p. 18.

logically. But is the Eucharist the holy celebration of a holy Church? Has it always been understood as such? My concern for the pastoral question remains. But the deeper question needs to be faced, as only through a carefully researched answer to that question can we hope to discover a satisfying solution to the immediate needs of people who suffer exclusion from the eucharistic table, which they long to share.

The most important starting-place in any search for the 'original base of meaning' is the authoritative and revealed 'Word of God' of the Bible. However, any serious Christian scholar must interpret the Bible within the Christian tradition, and here we are facing one of the most serious contemporary difficulties of Catholic theology and theologians. How does one creatively read the Word of God as it is revealed to us in the Scriptures while remaining loyal to the authentic tradition of the Catholic Church?

The issue I am investigating through this study is on the cutting edge of that question. The Law of the Catholic Church is quite clear on the matter. Anyone who is in a state of sin must not approach the Eucharist. Indeed, at the level of practice, while compassion should be shown to the sinner, the reception of the Eucharist is forbidden. The final articulation of this 'tradition' through the Code of Canon Law, however, is not just the result of the whims of the Canon Lawyers. On the contrary, what they have attempted to incorporate through these clear pieces of legislation is a long-respected 'tradition' in the Catholic Church.

Does this 'tradition' reflect what the New Testament has to say about Jesus' presence to his disciples in the Eucharist? A response can be sought in the eucharistic passages from the four gospels, and Paul's teaching in 1 Corinthians 10 and 11. I am raising an urgent question, which calls for some clarification upon the role the Word of God must play in its relationship with the traditions of the Church.[13]

One fact must be stated clearly. The difficult balance between the word of the Scriptures and the living tradition of the Church can be preserved only when full consideration and respect is given to each in its uniqueness, made evident in our respect for the importance of both, in their mutuality. To use Scripture brutally in an attempt to demolish later doctrines and piety, or to use later pious practices and doctrines brutally to create forced interpretations of the New Testament, damages the Church's presence as the sign and bearer of God's love. Exaggerations in either direction lead to a blinkered, and therefore impoverished, understanding of the richness of Christian

---

[13] This question has been faced by the fine essay of D. N. Power, 'The Holy Spirit: Scripture, Tradition and Interpretation', in G. Wainwright (ed.), *Keeping the Faith: Essays to Mark the Centenary of Lux Mundi* (London: SPCK, 1989) pp. 152–78.

tradition in its wholeness. This is so because such methods offend against the essential and delicate mutuality of Scripture and tradition, which, together, both create and nourish the Christian faith.

A New Testament analysis of one of the mysteries of our faith must always be aware of, and reflect, this mutuality. At no stage should it presuppose later dogmas, as it must always attempt to respect the literary and historical contexts of the documents and passages analysed while keeping a critical eye on the traditions that have been formed at a later stage. To ignore them would be, I believe, to fail as a scholar working within the Christian tradition. But what is the task of the Catholic exegete who must reflect upon data that sometimes questions widely accepted ideas and practices?[14]

Although it is clearly one of the most difficult aspects of the theological and pastoral task, it is essential that the Catholic Church pursue the challenge to learn from both of the sources that nourish her faith: Scripture and tradition. The temptation is always with us to lean more heavily on one or other side of these two sources for our life and practice of the Christian faith. We have a tendency to make a choice. Rather than looking to Scripture *and* tradition, we set up a conflict between Scripture *or* tradition.

The Second Vatican Council's Dogmatic Constitution on Divine Revelation spoke eloquently on the importance of this question:

> In the supremely wise arrangement of God, sacred Tra-
> dition, sacred Scripture and the Magisterium of the Church are
> so connected and associated that one of them cannot stand
> without the others. Working together, each in its own way
> under the action of the Holy Spirit, they all contribute effec-
> tively to the salvation of souls. (*Dei Verbum* 10: see paras 7–10)

While the principles stated in *Dei Verbum* 10 are clear, the exact nature of the relationship that should exist between Scripture and tradition has never been easy to either define or practise. The Council addressed the question, calling for interaction and mutuality in the following important statement:

> Sacred Tradition and Sacred Scripture, then, are bound
> closely together, and communicate one with the other. For
> both of them, flowing from the same divine well-spring, *come*

---

[14] On this question, see the brief but helpful reflections of I. de la Potterie, 'Principles for the Christian Interpretation of Sacred Scripture', in *The Hour of Jesus: The Passion and Resurrection of Jesus according to John: Text and Spirit* (Slough: St Paul Publications, 1989) pp. 182–90. See also R. E. Brown, 'Critical Biblical Exegesis and the Develop-ment of Doctrine', in *Biblical Exegesis and Church Doctrine* (New York: Paulist Press, 1985) pp. 26–53; F. J. Moloney, 'Whither Catholic Biblical Studies?', *Australasian Catholic Record* 66 (1989) 83–93.

together in some fashion to form one thing and move towards the same goal. (*Dei Verbum* 9. My emphasis.)

As the stressed words in my citation of the text of *Dei Verbum* 9 indicate, the fact of the mutuality is affirmed, but what precisely is meant by 'come together in some fashion' (Latin original: *in unum quodammodo coalescunt*)? This formula was deliberately left vague in the light of possible future ecumenical developments, but it leads to difficulties in understanding how Scripture and tradition relate to one another. R. Schnackenburg, the celebrated Catholic biblical scholar, has written of this Conciliar statement: 'This formulation was a compromise that was devised to keep the way to ecumenical dialogue open, but it is quite unsatisfactory. The expression requires a much broader theological treatment.'[15]

The Council document itself reflects the difficulties and tensions that have always existed between Scripture and tradition. Yet Vatican II, despite the difficulties it had in finding the exact formula, has taught that Scripture and tradition need one another, even though neither is totally at ease with the other. Tradition alone is insufficient,[16] but Scripture alone can also lead us into a blind alley.[17] The exact nature of the relationship between them remains the subject of theological debate, and no doubt the difficulties that the Conciliar statement has created will eventually produce a more exact understanding of this delicate relationship.

Theology, however, must look to the experience of the centuries. Experience teaches us that we have Christian Scriptures today because tradition has kept them alive. Tradition leads us to proclaim the Word of God in our liturgies, to use it for prayer and to find in it a programme for authentic Christian living. This happens today because it has happened in the Christian Churches for almost two thousand years. As is well known, Christian tradition was alive

[15] R. Schnackenburg, 'Die Funktion der Exegese in Theologie und Kirche', in *Massstab des Glaubens: Fragen heutiger Christen im Licht des Neuen Testaments* (Freiburg: Herder, 1978) p. 20. See, for a fuller critical discussion of this vague statement, J. Ratzinger, 'The Transmission of Divine Revelation', in H. Vorgrimler (ed.), *Commentary on the Documents of Vatican II* (London: Burns & Oates/Herder & Herder, 1967–69) vol. III, pp. 190–6.

[16] Alessandro Manzoni, the author of a famous Italian novel that in so many ways defends traditional values, nevertheless has his story-teller wisely comment: 'And you know that traditions alone, unless you help them, always say too little' (*I Promessi Sposi: Storia Milanese del Secolo XVII* [ed. Fausto Ghisalberti; Milano: Ulrico Hoepli, 1973] ch. 38:48 — my translation).

[17] Important contributions on the limitations of *sola Scriptura* are nowadays made by Protestant scholars. See, for example, P. Stuhlmacher, *Historical Criticism and Theological Interpretation of Scripture* (London: SPCK, 1977); J. Barr, *The Scope and Authority of the Bible* (Explorations in Theology 7; London: SCM Press, 1980).

before there was ever a New Testament. It was precisely the desire to 'write' some of the living tradition that led to the formation of the New Testament. Thus it is quite clear that tradition gave birth to the Gospel, and tradition keeps it alive in the heart of the Church.[18]

However, experience also teaches that tradition can fall into the temptation of becoming an end unto itself. It runs the danger of rendering absolute a particular cultural expression of the faith or a particular historical period in the life of the Church. This temptation stands behind many of the current difficulties from the conservative side of the Church today, which, in one way or another, refuses to live in a post-Vatican II Church. For example, Archbishop Marcel Lefebvre will not accept that the Church can understand itself or present itself to the world in any other way than that regulated by the teachings of the Councils of Trent and Vatican I. He has made particular historical and cultural expressions into an absolute.[19]

It is the double-edged sword of the Word of God 'piercing to the division of soul and spirit, of joints and marrow, and discerning the thoughts and intentions of the heart' (Heb. 4:12), which has always been used to remind the institution of the Church why she was instituted in the first place. Although tradition gave birth to the Scriptures, and keeps them alive in the Church, the Scriptures have the task of acting like a double-edged sword, bringing comfort to the afflicted and affliction to the comfortable, when the traditions have been exaggeratedly domesticated.

One of the best-known examples of this thorn-in-the-side presence of the challenge of the Word of God was the phenomenon of so-called earliest 'monks' in Egypt. They followed the lead of Antony, who responded to Jesus' words as they are recorded in the Gospel of Matthew: 'If you would be perfect, go sell what you possess and give to the poor, and you will have treasure in heaven' (Matt. 19:21).[20] Antony began a movement that, in the fourth century, led remarkable numbers of simple peasant people into the desert in an attempt to live the life that had been described in the early chapters of the Acts of the Apostles. This movement was (among many other things) a 'protest', based on the Word of God,

---

[18] There are many good books on this. For my own treatment, see F. J. Moloney, *The Living Voice of the Gospel: The Gospels Today* (Melbourne: Collins Dove, 1986) pp. 18–23.

[19] In Australia, powerful figures have also adopted a similar, but more politically nuanced, approach. See, for example, B. A. Santamaria, 'A Kingdom Divided Against Itself', *AD2000* 1 (April 1988) 4–7; Idem, 'The path to hell paved by theologians', *Australian*, Tuesday, 17 December 1988, p. 9. See the perceptive remarks on this issue by A. Gill, 'Rooting out heresy', *Time Australia* (9 January 1989) pp. 33–4.

[20] See R. C. Gregg (ed.), *Athanasius: The Life of Antony and the Letter to Marcellinus* (Classics of Western Spirituality; London: SPCK, 1980) pp. 30–2.

against the gradual assimilation of the Church into the bosom of Roman Imperial society after Constantine. Although somewhat of an overstatement, a leading contemporary historian of the early Church, W. H. C. Frend, has described Antony's movement into the desert: 'Almost for the first time in three centuries the Lord's commands were being accepted literally by Christ's followers.'[21]

In the midst of the continuing theological discussions on this important question, the experience of how Scripture and tradition have in fact related over the centuries teaches an important lesson. While the tradition keeps the Scriptures alive in the Church, Scripture keeps the tradition honest.[22] I have written this study on the basis of this axiom.

Is our current tradition of the admission only of the 'worthy' to our eucharistic celebrations in need of the corrective word of the Scriptures to keep it honest? I am raising a question to an important aspect of the Church's pastoral practice, a practice that has become so much a part of the Church's life that it is in her Canon Law. Does this practice of excluding those judged as being sinful, for whatever reason, reflect an understanding of the Church celebrating Eucharist that is faithful to the authoritative Word of God as it has come down to us in the Scriptures? Indeed, we need to reach farther back, behind the witness of the gospels and ask: is our present practice loyal to Jesus' own teaching and practice?[23]

Posing Questions to the Tradition

It is important to appreciate the corrective role that a careful reading of the word of the Scriptures plays in the heart of the Church. Of course, it is only one of the many roles that the Word of God must play. It is not its most important role. First of all, the Word of God nourishes, inspires and guides us. As the Second Vatican Council has told us:

> The Church has always venerated the divine Scriptures as she venerated the Body of the Lord, in so far as she never ceases, particularly in the sacred liturgy, to partake of the bread of life and to offer it to the faithful from the one table of the Word of God and the Body of Christ. (*Dei Verbum* 21)

---

[21] W. H. C. Frend, *The Rise of Christianity* (London: Darton, Longman & Todd, 1984) p. 423.

[22] See, on this, Moloney, *Living Voice*, pp. 223–43.

[23] As Power, 'Holy Spirit', p. 167 comments: 'In attending to what is proclaimed from the Bible, or to what is celebrated in liturgy, or to what is passed on in tradition, the Church needs to listen keenly for a word that speaks from a deeper experience of redemption than do the paradigmatic patterns of speech adopted from patriarchal, hierarchical or technological cultures.'

The 'corrective' role of the Scriptures must be seen and understood within the wider and more positive terms so beautifully stated in the teaching of the Council. Only from its position side by side with the Eucharist itself, nourishing a people from the one Table of the Lord, may we allow the Scriptures to raise questions. What we are attempting through this study is to further purify, deepen and enrich our contemporary understanding and practice of the Eucharist.[24]

There is a need to question an aspect of our current traditions by looking at the foundational eucharistic passages in the Scriptures. I will devote my attention to the narratives of the two feeding miracles in the Gospel of Mark and of Matthew, and to Luke's remodelling of the two miracle stories into one single account. I will necessarily study the accounts of the last meal between Jesus and his disciples found in all three Synoptic Gospels (Mark, Matthew and Luke) and to the special Lucan story of the walk to Emmaus. Beyond the Synoptic tradition, there is need to look at both the Pauline and the Johannine practice and understanding of the Eucharist as reflected in their own special use of the meal that Jesus celebrated with his disciples.

Many studies of the eucharistic material in the New Testament attempt historical reconstruction. Oceans of ink have been spent attempting to rediscover exactly what happened on that night. Was it a Passover meal? What were the exact words that Jesus said over the bread and then over the cup (if he used a cup)? Which of the two major traditions: Mark and Matthew (Jerusalem tradition) or Luke and Paul (Antiochene tradition) is the more primitive?[25] These, and many similar questions, have never been finally resolved. The study that follows, although presupposing much of the work that has been done on the historical background to our eucharistic texts, does not ask such questions.[26]

---

[24] de la Potterie, *Hour of Jesus*, p. 157, puts it very well: 'Faithfulness to tradition does not consist in merely repeating what has already been said, but in following and extending the dynamic of a movement. With the new means at our disposal it is a question of carrying the tradition still further. Every epoch is a link in the chain of a living tradition, in a process that will continue right to the parousia.'

[25] The classical study along these lines remains that of J. Jeremias, *The Eucharistic Words of Jesus* (London: SCM Press, 1966). A more satisfactory approach to the same questions is adopted by X. Léon-Dufour, *Sharing the Eucharistic Bread: The Witness of the New Testament* (New York: Paulist Press, 1987), pp. 183–202. This is the most important contemporary work on the New Testament eucharistic texts. See my review of the French edition in *Catholic Biblical Quarterly* 46 (1984) 350–2.

[26] For a very useful overview of the study of the historical question from the beginnings of the century until 1986, see J. Kodell, *The Eucharist in the New Testament* (Zacchaeus Studies: New Testament; Wilmington: Michael Glazier, 1989) pp. 22–37.

This study is deliberately limited to a consideration of the theological and religious message of the present structure of the gospels and of 1 Corinthians 10–11. I am asking what we can learn from the rediscovery of the eucharistic thought and practice of the Marcan Church, the Matthean Church, the Lucan Church, the Johannine Church and the Christians in Corinth. As I have already mentioned, this is not the only way in which one can approach these texts. It may not even be the best way. However, it is important to ask these questions of the foundational New Testament Churches.

The Evangelists and the Apostle Paul received traditions concerning the meal that Jesus shared with his disciples on the night before he died (see especially 1 Cor. 11:23, where this is explicitly stated). Not one of them repeated a single fixed text in which every word was sacred and irreplaceable. They knew that they must speak the living word in a way that translated its deepest message to the needs of the various ecclesial communities.[27]

Research into what may have been the original event that took place between Jesus and his disciples must base itself on these texts 'translated' to meet the needs of the various ecclesial communities. No doubt the discovery of exactly when the meal took place, the exact words and gestures used on that occasion and the subsequent transmission of this data is important. An indication of the speculative nature of this difficult task is found in the fact that the two great experts in this area, Joachim Jeremias and Heinz Schürmann, have given up their lifelong attempts to establish this data definitively.[28]

Less speculative, and *at least* equally as important, is the task of reading what each inspired author proclaims through the way he tells the story of Jesus. In fact, when it comes to the Eucharist, all the New Testament authors, including Paul, tell the story of Jesus' sharing a meal. This study turns its attention almost exclusively to the message of each of the Evangelists and Saint Paul.[29] A certain unity behind the thought of all of these authors from the early Church would force me to ask an historical question. Where did the early Church's understanding of the Church's eucharistic meals have its origin? If the same theme is expressed in a variety of ways across the whole of the New Testament, is it possible that it had its origins in the meals of Jesus himself?

---

[27] See Léon-Dufour, *Sharing*, pp. 181–2.

[28] For detail, see Léon-Dufour, *Sharing*, pp. 77–8 and 336, note 1. G. Martelet, *The Risen Christ and the Eucharistic World* (London: Collins, 1976) p. 97: 'It is in practice impossible to put forward a convincing *genealogy* of the texts.'

[29] For the importance of this 'narrative approach' to the Scriptures, see Power, 'Holy Spirit', pp. 168–70.

Conclusion

Over the years we have understood the Eucharist as the place of encounter between Jesus and the worthy, yet the analysis of the Word of God that follows seems to show that it is the place of encounter between Jesus and the broken sinners. Jesus' eucharistic presence is for his failed and failing disciples. However, the theology of discipleship in the New Testament does not primarily present the celebration of the Eucharist as an encounter between Jesus and the broken, sinful *individual Christian*. In Mark, Matthew, Luke, John and Paul it is with a broken Church that the Lord breaks the bread of his body. Disciples in the Gospel stories are not just founding figures from the distant past. They represent the Church of all times. It is in the experience of the disciples of the Gospel stories that the disciples of the twentieth and twenty-first century will discover their own experience of faith and sinfulness.

Although studies of this nature may be something of a thorn in the side to some Catholics,[30] critical reflection upon our New Testament tradition is a service that a professional scholar is called to offer the Church.[31] The task of being an academic in the Catholic Church today brings its difficulties,[32] but the task must be carried on for the continued life of the Church. Without it, we run the risk of falling into a stagnant dogmatism. As Raymond Brown has written: 'Even when finally fixed in a formula, tradition does not stifle further insight derived from a deeper penetration of Scripture.'[33]

The 'questioning' of traditional practices through a careful use of the Scriptures is a delicate but necessary task in a human institution that always runs the risk of the 'distortion' of its traditions. In his

---

[30] For example, in response to a public lecture that I had given, David Kehoe (*Advocate*, Thursday, 1 December 1988, p. 2) offers his own appreciation of the gospels, accusing me of 'a failure to recognise all the historical details of a Gospel account' and closes by submitting 'that, objectively, Fr Moloney is neither accurate, nor properly informed, nor fostering dialogue with fidelity'. The *Advocate* is the Melbourne Catholic weekly newspaper.

[31] One of the difficulties is that, through all the questioning and the necessary scientific hypotheses, the theologian stands by the teaching and the practice demanded by the Magisterium. As the great theologians of our century have shown (Lagrange, de Chardin, de Lubac and Congar: all of whom were 'silenced'), such behaviour is generally the ultimate test of the 'truth' of their claims.

[32] These difficulties arise from many sides. It is often felt that we put at risk the 'simple faith' of the so-called ordinary people. Australians recently witnessed the termination of the popular column written by Fr Bill O'Shea in the *Catholic Leader* for these reasons. For detail, see the *Catholic Leader*, 26 July 1987. Objections are also raised for seemingly scholarly reasons. See, for example, D. Farkasfalvy, 'In Search of a "post-critical" method of biblical interpretation for Catholic theology', *Communio* 13 (1986) 288–307.

[33] Brown, 'Critical Biblical Exegesis', p. 33.

commentary on the difficult paragraph of *Dei Verbum* already mentioned (*Dei Verbum* 9), Joseph Ratzinger raises the urgency of the need
to face these 'distortions' with the correcting role of the scriptures:

> We shall have to acknowledge the truth of the criticism
> that there is, in fact, no explicit mention of the possibility of a
> distorting tradition and of the place of Scripture as an element
> within the Church that is *also* critical of tradition, which
> means that a most important side of the problem, as shown by
> the history of the Church — and perhaps the real crux of the
> *ecclesia semper reformanda* — has been overlooked . . . That this
> opportunity has been missed can only be regarded as an
> unfortunate omission.[34]

In a later article in the same volume, commenting on *Dei Verbum*
23, Ratzinger writes:

> A reference to the ecclesial nature of exegesis, on the one
> hand, and to its methodological correctness on the other, again
> expresses the inner tension of Church exegesis, which can no
> longer be removed, *but must be simply accepted as tension*.[35] (My
> emphasis.)

It is within this tension that we must stand, not trying to ease
away its pain by either a rigid and unbending dogmatism or by an
uncritical and unfounded 'change for the sake of change' approach.[36]
I am aware that the exegete can never hope to resolve this difficult
problem. It is a task that the whole Church, under the guidance of
the Magisterium, must face. Yet the question that I wish to raise is
basic. Has the tradition on the issue of the presence of the Lord to
the broken in our celebration of the Eucharist been 'distorted'
(Ratzinger)?

---

[34] Ratzinger, 'Transmission of Divine Revelation', pp. 192–3.

[35] 'Sacred Scripture in the Life of the Church', in H. Vorgrimler (ed.), *Commentary on the Documents of Vatican II*, vol. 3, p. 268.

[36] I agree with Brown, 'Critical Biblical Exegesis', p. 52: 'Neither a fundamentalist interpretation of the NT, which finds later dogmas with great clarity in the NT era, nor a liberal view, which rejects anything which goes beyond Jesus, is faithful to Catholic history.'

CHAPTER TWO

The Gospel
of Mark

The four gospels are basically the story of the life, teaching, death and resurrection of Jesus, told through the careful gathering together and ordering of many smaller stories that came to the Evangelists. We cannot look to them as textbooks that will provide us with abstract discussions about Jesus and the Eucharist.[1] As stories, however, they have their own powerful way of instructing. The genuine teaching of the Evangelists can be found through the narratives, the use of symbols and metaphors, the deliberate ordering of the material of the story itself and many other features that are characteristics of 'story'.

Thus, in our search to discover what Mark (and indeed Matthew, Luke and John) wanted to say about the Eucharist, we must pay close attention to the very fabric of his particular approach to telling the story of Jesus of Nazareth.[2] In this way we will be able to detect

---

[1] For a description of how the gospels came to be, and how one should approach them, see Moloney, *Living Voice*, pp. 3–23 (the chapter entitled 'Reading a Gospel Today').

[2] Another way to approach Mark's particular point of view is to trace his own contributions to the traditions that came to him. This can be a very speculative task, and I am using a different approach. However, a recent work dedicated to this issue has shown considerable Marcan activity in the passages we are considering. See E. J. Pryke, *Redactional Style in the Marcan Gospel: A Study of Syntax and Vocabulary as Guides to Redaction in Mark* (SNTS Monograph Series 33; Cambridge (UK): Cambridge University Press, 1978) pp. 159–60, 162, 171–2.

what the experience of Eucharist meant for Mark and his community. Indeed, perhaps with Mark we might find that members of his community had lost their way in understanding the Eucharist, and that the Evangelist uses the 'stories' of his Gospel both to summon them to a more committed Christian life, and to comfort them in their difficulties and failures.[3]

The Disciples

Among the many features of any narrative there are two crucial elements, without which there would be no 'story':
(a) the characters or players in the drama;[4]
(b) the plot within which they act out their part.[5]
The Gospel of Mark is famous for its portrait of the disciples of Jesus. Apart from Jesus, obviously the leading character in the plot, the disciples are the main protagonists in this Gospel. A literary critic, writing in general of protagonists in a narrative, has described Mark's disciples well. They are:

> ... the vehicles by which all the most interesting questions are raised; they evoke our beliefs, sympathies, revulsions; they incarnate the moral vision of the world inherent in the total novel. In a sense they are what the novel exists for; it exists to reveal them.[6]

Jesus' disciples, according to Mark's Gospel, share in a privileged way in Jesus' person and mission. They respond immediately to the 'call' to follow Jesus (1:16–20, 2:13–14). They witness the wonders that he does, and they also receive private instruction from him (4:11, 34; 7:17; 9:1–10). The Twelve are called to 'be with him', so that they might participate in the spread of God's reign by preaching and having authority to cast out demons (3:13–15). They are formally sent out on that mission by Jesus himself (6:7–12). If we had only this side of the story, it would be clear that Mark wished to use the disciples as models for those privileged to be called to the Christian life. We, the readers, would be happy to associate ourselves with this success story. There could be a sympathetic association between the 'disciples of Jesus', who play a leading role in the

---

[3] I have been helped in the reflections that follow, especially concerning Mark 6:31–44 and 8:1–10, by D. Senior, 'The Eucharist in Mark: Mission, Reconciliation, Hope', *Biblical Theology Bulletin* 12 (1982) 67–72.

[4] See, on the characters in the Gospel of Mark, D. Rhoads & D. Michie, *Mark as Story: An Introduction to the Narrative of a Gospel* (Philadelphia: Fortress Press, 1982) pp. 101–36.

[5] See, on the plot of the Gospel of Mark, Rhoads & Michie, *Mark as Story*, pp. 73–100.

[6] W. J. Harvey, *Character and the Novel* (London: Chatto & Windus, 1965) p. 56.

Gospel of Mark and the 'disciples of Jesus' who are reading the narrative of the Gospel.

But, such is not the case. W. J. Harvey wrote of the possibility that characters in a narrative can create a reaction of 'revulsion' in the reader.[7] What is surprising about the disciples in the Gospel of Mark is that as the story of Jesus progresses, the failure of the disciples increases. Indeed, the disciples consistently fail in the Gospel of Mark. They fail to understand his parables (4:13; see also 7:18) and his miracles (4:40–41). On returning from their mission, they are anxious to tell Jesus all the things that *they* had said and done (6:30). They are unable to understand Jesus' walking on the seas (6:51–52). They want to set up an exclusive discipleship, and are hostile to others who do not see things their way (9:38–41; 10:13–16). Across the central section of the Gospel, as Jesus' movement towards death and Jerusalem becomes explicit (8:22–10:52), Jesus speaks three times of his oncoming passion, and each time the disciples either fail or refuse to understand (8:32; 9:32–34; 10:35–45).[8] While this may not produce 'revulsion' in the reader, the disciples are certainly not the heroes of the narrative.

The failure of the disciples comes to a head in the passion story. Judas, 'one of the Twelve', betrays Jesus (14:10–11), Peter denies him (14:66–72) and his most intimate followers, Peter, James and John, sleep through his hour of agonising prayer (14:32–42). Their final exit from the story is found in 14:50: 'And they all forsook him, and fled.' This is the last appearance of the disciples in the Gospel of Mark and their flight immediately receives comment in the brief parabolic narrative that Mark reports. There was also a young man 'following'. He, too, at the threat of danger, fled, leaving the only covering that he had on his body, a linen cloth, in the hands of his assailants. Like the disciples who have just fled, he is naked in his nothingness.

There are no disciples at the cross of Jesus in Mark's Gospel. Nor, surprisingly, are they found in his brief resurrection story (16:1–8).[9] There are, however, hints of an eventual restoration to their place 'following' Jesus. The flight of the disciples is marked by the parallel

---

[7] See previous note.

[8] On this whole section, see Moloney, *Living Voice*, pp. 27–42.

[9] Mark 16:9–20, found in many Bibles, was added to the Gospel. As the note to the passage in *The New Jerusalem Bible* (London: Darton, Longman & Todd, 1985) p. 1685 explains: 'The longer ending of Mk, vv. 9–20 is included in the canonically accepted body of inspired scripture, although some important MSS omit it, and it does not seem to be by Mark. It is in a different style, and is little more than a summary of the appearances of the risen Christ, with other material, all of which could be derived from various NT writings.' I maintain that the original Gospel ended at 16:8. On this, see N. Perrin, *The Resurrection Narratives: A New Approach* (London: SCM Press, 1977) pp. 20–2.

flight of a young man, naked in his nothingness, but at the empty
tomb the women find 'a young man, sitting on the right side,
dressed in a white robe' (16:5). They are then commissioned: 'Go
tell his disciples and Peter that he is going before you to Galilee;
there you will see him, as he told you' (v. 7).

Has Mark used Jesus' disciples as characters to arouse 'belief,
sympathy or revulsion'? Scholars have interpreted this evidence in
the Gospel in a variety of ways. Many claim that, for Mark, the
disciples offer no paradigm for the Marcan Church or for the Church
of any age, as they fail and thus create only 'revulsion'. As one of
these scholars has put it:

> I conclude that Mark is assiduously involved in a ven-
> detta against the disciples. He paints them as obtuse, obdurate,
> recalcitrant men who at first are unperceptive of Jesus' mes-
> siahship, then oppose its style and character, and finally totally
> reject it. As a *coup de grâce*, Mark closes his Gospel without
> rehabilitating the disciples.[10]

This widely held position throws into relief the failure, but
underplays and misunderstands the importance of the positive side
of the disciples' story. The two must be held in tension, and there is
a need to stress both the positive and the negative in the story of the
disciples, as it is the story of all disciples.[11] For Mark it is especially
the story of his own community, a community of (failing?) disciples.

The Gospel of Mark reveals disciples for what they are. The
failure of the disciples is a message about the overpowering need for
dependence upon Jesus, and trust in God's saving power through
him. Discipleship is a mixture of privilege and egoism, of success
and failure. Mark has understood this well from his experience of
discipleship in the Church. He has thus, in the telling of his Gospel
story, addressed the problem of the ambiguity of Christian disciples
through his use of Jesus' own first disciples.[12]

They did not understand about the loaves

It is against the background of Mark's broader canvas of the
disciples throughout the whole of Jesus' story that we must approach the accounts of Jesus' multiplication of the loaves and fishes.

---

[10] T. J. Weeden, *Mark — Traditions in Conflict* (Philadelphia: Fortress Press, 1976)
pp. 50–1.

[11] See especially R. C. Tannehill, 'The Disciples in Mark: The Function of a Narrative
Role', *Journal of Religion* 57 (1977) 386–405.

[12] For a survey of the various scholarly positions on Marcan discipleship, see
F. J. Moloney, 'The Vocation of the Disciples in the Gospel of Mark', *Salesianum* 43
(1981) 488–95 (the whole article: pp. 487–515).

There are important eucharistic teachings in Mark's two accounts of the multiplication of the bread and the feeding of the multitudes (Mark 6:31–44; 8:1–10).[13] But we need to stand back from the stories themselves, to trace their position within the 'plot' of Mark's narrative structure. An injustice would be done to Mark and his message if we were simply to concentrate our attention upon the detail of the two passages. We are not only interested in the possible eucharistic material that one may or may not be able to find in the details of the miracle stories in themselves. What is more important, for our purposes, is to understand how Mark used these eucharistic stories within his overall plot. 'Plot' has been described by M. H. Abrams as follows: 'The plot in a dramatic or narrative work is the structure of its actions, as these are ordered and rendered toward achieving particular emotional and artistic effects.'[14]

In our approach to Mark 6:31–44 and 8:1–10, we need to watch for hints in the wider context of the whole story. To understand this, we will survey 'the structure of the actions' of the first half of the Gospel. We need only trace the plot as far as its mid-point, as all commentators agree that Peter's confession of Jesus as the Christ (8:27–30) forms the central piece of Mark's literary structure. The first half of the Gospel moves towards a confession of Jesus as the Christ, and the second half, culminating in the death and resurrection of Jesus, will explain what such a confession means.

The Gospel begins with a prologue to the life and teaching of Jesus (1:1–13). The reader thus begins the narrative of the Gospel proper informed that Jesus of Nazareth is 'the Christ, the Son of God' (vv. 1, 11), witnessed to by God himself (vv. 2–3), full of and directed by the Spirit (vv. 10, 12). In the desert, ministered to by the angels and 'with the wild beasts', he is also a sign of a renewal of God's original created order.[15]

The Evangelist then reports, in brief and powerful summary, Jesus' bursting on the scene and preaching the Gospel (1:14–15). This is followed by the call of the first disciples (1:16–20). As the public ministry of Jesus opens, he overcomes the evil of sickness and devil possession (1:21–45), but finds unresolved conflict in the official representatives of Israel (2:1–3:6). This part of the Gospel concludes in 3:6: 'The Pharisees went out and immediately held

---

[13] For a critical assessment of this question, see R. M. Fowler, *Loaves and Fishes: The Function of the Feeding Stories in the Gospel of Mark* (SBL Dissertation Series 54; Chico: Scholars Press, 1981) pp. 132–47.

[14] M. H. Abrams, *A Glossary of Literary Terms* (New York: Holt, Reinhart & Winston, 1988) p. 139.

[15] For this perspective, see M. D. Hooker, *The Message of Mark* (London: Epworth Press, 1983) pp. 1–16.

counsel with the Herodians against him, how to destroy him.'

A further summary of Jesus' ministry is again found at the opening of the next section (3:7–12), and this is also followed by discipleship material. This time it is the calling and commissioning of the Twelve, where Jesus forms a 'new family', calling them 'to be with him' and to share in his life and mission (3:13–19a). The narrative then tells of the inability of both Jesus' physical family and his cultural and religious family to understand and accept him (3:19b–35). Through a series of parables (4:1–34) and miracles (4:35–5:43) Jesus preaches the kingdom, and demonstrates the power of its presence. However, on his return to 'his own country' (6:1), his people ask the right questions about the origin of his wisdom and power, but they give the wrong answer: 'Is this not the carpenter, the son of Mary?' (see 6:2–3). Jesus is amazed at their unbelief (6:6a). A 'new family' has been created now: 'Whoever does the will of God is my brother and sister and mother' (3:35).

Having met opposition from Israel, and then from 'his own', he now turns decisively to his disciples. Again the section begins with a summary of Jesus' activity (6:6b) and further discipleship material, as he sends out his disciples 'two by two' into the mission (6:7–13). The following narrative (solemnly concluded with another decision about Jesus: Peter's confession 'You are the Christ' (8:29)) is highlighted by the two feeding miracles. While 1:14–3:6 featured Jesus and his encounter with Israel, and 3:7–6:6a the encounter between Jesus and 'his own', 6:6b–8:30 focuses its attention on that 'new family' of the disciples, which had already been established through vocation (1:16–20) and commissioning (3:13–19).

One of the major features of Mark 6:6b–8:30, a section of the Gospel particularly interested in the 'new family' of Jesus, is the twofold feeding miracle. Starting our analysis with this seeming repetition of an almost identical miracle, it is important to observe that after both miracles Mark indicates that the disciples failed to understand. Immediately after the first feeding, Jesus comes to them on the water (6:45–52). However, despite all they have experienced, the disciples fail to grasp the meaning of Jesus' manifestation of himself. 'And he got into the boat with them and the wind ceased. And they were utterly astounded, for they did not understand about the loaves, but their hearts were hardened' (6:52).

After the second feeding story the disciples set out across the lake with Jesus. He speaks to them about 'the leaven' of the Pharisees (8:15), but the disciples presume he is making reference to the 'one loaf' that they have on board (8:14). Jesus then speaks strongly to them, recalling *both* the feeding miracles:

> Jesus said to them, 'Why do you discuss the fact that you have no bread? Do you not yet perceive or understand? Are

your hearts hardened? Having eyes do you not see, and having ears do you not hear? And do you not remember? When I broke the five loaves for the five thousand, how many baskets full of broken pieces did you take up?' They said to him, 'Twelve'. 'And the seven for the four thousand, how many baskets full of fragments did you collect?' And they said to him, 'Seven'. And he said to them, 'Do you not yet understand?' (8:17–21)

It is against this background of the disciples' lack of understanding that we must interpret Mark's telling of the feeding stories of 6:31–44 and 8:1–10. Many elements in these stories have close contacts with the celebration of the Eucharist.[16] The actions of Jesus in both stories — 'taking' the loaves, 'looking up to heaven', 'giving thanks', 'breaking bread' and 'giving' it to the disciples (see 6:41 and 8:6) are obvious links with the actual celebration of Eucharist in the Marcan community. The Greek word used for 'fragments' (*klasmata*) is an important eucharistic term in later texts.[17]

These accounts reflect the Marcan community, aware of the nourishment that the encounter with the eucharistic Lord provides. Yet the Lord himself does not make the distribution. That is a task that has been given to the disciples themselves. In the first miracle, seeing the lonely place and the lateness of the hour, the disciples ask Jesus to send the multitude away to the surrounding villages to buy themselves something to eat. Jesus replies: 'You give them something to eat' (6:37). After taking, blessing and breaking the loaves, Jesus 'gave them to the disciples to set before the people' (v. 41). The second miracle is inspired by Jesus' compassion for the crowd, which has 'come a very long way' (8:3). There is no command to the disciples to feed the people, but they are given the task. Again we read that Jesus 'gave them [the broken loaves] to his disciples to set before the people; and they set them before the crowd' (v. 6).

The feeding of the multitudes is a task that the disciples must perform. This partly explains why these two important stories are found precisely at this stage of Mark's 'plot'. Mark is concerned here to present Jesus' missioning of his disciples. The first miracle story (6:31–44) follows Jesus' sending out the Twelve on mission (6:7–13),

---

[16] On the eucharistic elements in the tradition, see S. Masuda, 'The Good News of the Miracle of the Bread: The Tradition and Its Markan Redaction', *New Testament Studies* 28 (1982) 201–3.

[17] For a detailed study of the process that led from a feeding miracle in the life of Jesus to the Marcan eucharistic re-fashioning of that story, see J.-M. van Cangh, *La Multiplication des pains et l'Eucharistie* (Lectio Divina 86; Paris: Editions du Cerf, 1975) pp. 67–109. See also B. van Iersel, 'Die wunderbare Speisung und das Abendmahl in der synoptischen Tradition (Mk VI 35–44 par., VIII 1–20 par.)', *Novum Testamentum 7* (1964) 167–94, and Masuda, 'Good News', 191–219.

and a lengthy description of the death of John the Baptist (6:14–29), which hints that such will be the destiny of all who are prepared to take the risk of following Jesus down *his* way. After this interlude, the disciples return from the mission, full of their *own* importance and success (6:30). The feeding story that now follows (6:31–44) is set within *Jewish* territory, but the question of the mission of the disciples has already been seriously raised in all the material that immediately preceded it (vv. 7–30).

The mission again emerges powerfully between the first and the second feeding accounts (7:1–30). The passage opens with a polemical encounter between Jesus and Israel (7:1–23). The point at issue is 'eating'. The verb 'to eat' (Greek *esthiein*) and the word for 'bread' (Greek *artos*) highlight the conflict (see 7:2, 3, 4, 5). While Israel judges 'eating' by 'what is outside' (vv. 15 and 18), the real causes of sinfulness are to be found elsewhere. There is a list of vices given in vv. 21–22, which 'come from within' (v. 23). Some of these are to be expected, as they come from the decalogue, but there are further vices, which 'separate' people: envy, slander, pride and foolishness. While Israel uses external criteria for assessing ritual cleanliness, Jesus points out that lasting divisions are created by much more profound defects. Writing to his own community, is Mark warning the people against their own tendencies to be divided by envy, slander, pride and foolishness?[18]

Having posed this question, Jesus sets out on a journey that will always be in Gentile territory. So that the reader will make no mistake as to Jesus' presence in a Gentile world, Mark stresses the *geography* of Jesus' movements: 'And from there he arose and went away to the region of Tyre and Sidon' (7:24), and: 'Then he returned from the region of Tyre and went through Sidon to the Sea of Galilee through the region of the Decapolis' (v. 31). On this journey through Gentile lands and peoples, Jesus cures a Syrophoenician woman's daughter and thus reverses the established order of those at table and those seeking the crumbs that fall (7:27).[19] Still in a Gentile land he cures a deaf mute, who immediately describes Jesus in terms that recall the prophet Isaiah's description of the Messiah (7:37; see Isaiah 35:5–6).

The second feeding, which now follows (8:1–10), is clearly set in *Gentile* territory. Thus, within an overall context of mission, Jesus

---

[18] I am grateful to Michael FitzPatrick, OFM, who posed this question to me.

[19] P. Esler, *Community and Gospel in Luke–Acts: The Social and Political Motivations of Lucan Theology* (SNTS Monograph Series 57; Cambridge (UK): Cambridge University Press, 1987) pp. 89–91 analyses Mark 7:1–30 and its understanding of food laws and table-fellowship. He concludes: 'We are surely meant to see this image as a justification for the eucharistic fellowship of Jews and Gentiles in the Christian community.'

himself feeds both Jews and Greeks.[20] What of the disciples in these feeding miracles? In both accounts they want to send the crowds away (6:35–36; 8:4). As we have already seen, Jesus will not allow this. He thus commands them: 'You give them something to eat' (6:37) and he involves them in the actual feeding (6:41, 8:6).

As throughout the Gospel, the disciples are called to a privileged participation in the mission of the Lord. In this case, it is a call to feed both the Jews and the Gentiles. But, as we have seen, 'they did not understand about the loaves'. The Church is for both Jew and Gentile, nourished by the disciples of Jesus, but the disciples do not understand. Indeed, they should have recalled that some of his earlier meals with them had overturned the barriers set up by the religious authorities to exclude some people from table-fellowship (see 2:15–17, 18–22). As Léon-Dufour has commented: 'Those surprising meals had symbolized in a transparent way the universality of his message: the reign of God that is at hand is available to every human being.'[21] But the disciples 'did not understand about the loaves'.

Mark has set the two accounts of Jesus' sending his disciples to feed both Jewish and Gentile multitudes at the heart of his story of the mission of the disciples. The disciples do not understand the bread, and they are unwilling to perform this task. They would prefer the people to look after themselves. Behind this narrative lie hidden the difficulties of the early Christian community over the mission to the Gentiles, no more profoundly felt than when it gathered for Eucharist. This section of Mark's Gospel reflects the pain that was keenly felt as many struggled both for and against the opening of the community's eucharistic table to both Jewish Christians and Gentile Christians. The problem of table-fellowship in the early Church was understandably widespread, and it is reflected in other parts of the New Testament (especially Acts 10–11 and Gal. 2:11–21).

The question of an 'exclusive' concept of presence at the eucharistic table stands behind these two feeding miracles, placed strategically within the whole context of 6:6b–8:30. Mark has told his story of the two miracles of feeding the multitudes to teach the members of his community that they were to share in the universal mission of Jesus, cost what it may (6:14–29: the death of John the Baptist). At the heart of that mission was eucharistic table-fellowship, which meant one bread for many different people, even those whom the original disciples would have liked to exclude from the table. Jesus,

---

[20] On the significance of the Jewish and Gentile feedings, see especially van Cangh, *La Multiplication*, pp. 111–31.

[21] Léon-Dufour, *Sharing*, p. 185.

taking from the poverty and insufficiency of the disciple's mere few loaves and fishes (6:41 and 8:6), feeds the multitudes on both the Jewish and the Gentile side of the lake.[22]

As the disciples in Jesus' story merited the stern words of Jesus (8:17–21) because they failed to understand the meaning of the loaves, the disciples of Mark's own community are being warned that they should be careful not to repeat such hardness of heart, such blindness in their exclusive understanding of the Lord's Table.

Jesus' Last Meal with his Disciples

We have seen an important eucharistic message in the Marcan bread stories for a Church of disciples that is struggling with the temptation to exclude people from the eucharistic table. Our attention can now turn to the most explicit eucharistic text in this Gospel: the Marcan version of the last meal that Jesus shared with these same disciples. Again we must trace Mark's very personal way of telling this story of the night before Jesus died, in close association with disciples who will either betray or deny him (14:17–31).[23]

Along with the use of characters, acting out their roles within a plot, contemporary narrative criticism is also pointing out the importance of seeing the 'rhetoric' of the narrative itself. While characters are the actors, and the plot is the placing of one event after another to create an impression and lead towards a conclusion, the rhetoric of a narrative is made up of the stylistic features that the author deliberately employs as he unfolds his plot.[24] Rhoads and Michie define these stylistic features as the literary devices used by the narrator 'to hold people's attention from one episode to another'.[25]

One of the features of Marcan style is the tendency to 'frame' stories. Very often the Evangelist will single out an important narrative and then frame it. This means that he opens a certain

---

[22] See van Iersel, 'Die wunderbare Speisung', pp. 186–90.

[23] Not all would see the section 14:17–31 as a unit. Some scholars separate vv. 26–31 from the Supper, because of the 'and they went out' in v. 26. See, for example, V. Taylor, *The Gospel According to St Mark* (London: Macmillan, 1966) p. 548; L. Williamson, *Mark* (Interpretation; Atlanta: John Knox Press, 1983) p. 257. Others separate vv. 27–31, linking v. 26 to vv. 22–25, as they see in the singing of the hymn (v. 26) a reference to the use of the second half of the Hallel Psalms as the conclusion to table-fellowship. See, for example, W. L. Lane, *Commentary on the Gospel of Mark* (New International Commentary on the NT; Grand Rapids: Eerdmans, 1974) pp. 509–10. As will soon be apparent, the overall plot of 14:1–72 demands my division.

[24] For an outline of the 'rhetoric' of the Gospel of Mark, see Rhoads & Michie, *Mark as Story*, pp. 35–62. See also H. C. Kee, *Community of the New Age: Studies in Mark's Gospel* (London: SCM Press, 1977) pp. 50–76.

[25] Rhoads & Michie, *Mark as Story*, p. 35.

narrative or theme, then breaks into it with another, quite different narrative, resuming his original theme or narrative once he has told his central piece. An example of this is the frame of Jairus summoning Jesus to come to his daughter (5:21–24) and the actual raising of Jairus' daughter (vv. 35–43) around the cure of the woman with the flow of blood (vv. 25–34). Another is the frame of Jesus' cursing of the fig tree (11:12–14) and the sight of the withered tree (vv. 20–21) around the story of Jesus' ending all business and cultic practices in the Temple in Jerusalem (vv. 15–19). The list could go on (see also 3:20–35; 6:7–30; 14:1–11, 54–72), as it is a structure dear to Mark.[26]

Sections of Mark's Gospel that are framed in this way must be interpreted as a whole. The sections that form the frame serve to explain the section framed, and vice versá. The experience of Jairus' daughter raised to life and the experience of the woman with the flow of blood restored to full life as a woman enrich the significance of each account.[27] Similarly, the barren fig tree and the fruitlessness of traditional Temple worship also needs to be interpreted around the one theme.

Once this aspect of Marcan 'rhetoric' is noticed, then we must interpret Mark 14:17–31 in this way. The Evangelist has told the central story of Jesus' final meal with his disciples (14:22–25) within the 'frame' of two narratives that predict their betrayal of him (vv. 17–21) and their abandoning him in flight (vv. 26–31).[28]

Before analysing the section of the Gospel contained within the unit of 14:17–31 we again need to look wider, to see whether there are further indications of Mark's 'plot'. It is most helpful to notice that the framed passage that interests us in a particular way forms part of a much wider literary pattern. The whole of Mark 14:1–72, dedicated to Jesus' last evening with his disciples, his prayer, his arrest and the Jewish trial, has been carefully constructed by the Evangelist Mark. Throughout this opening section of the passion narrative, Mark has deliberately situated accounts that tell of what

---

[26] On this, see Kee, *Community*, pp. 54–6; Rhoads & Michie, *Mark as Story*, p. 51, and especially J. R. Donahue, *Are You the Christ? The Trial Narrative in the Gospel of Mark* (SBL Dissertation Series 10; Missoula: Scholars Press, 1973) pp. 57–63. It is often presupposed that Mark was too naïve an author to have used such skilful techniques. Donahue's response to this point of view is: 'The present work moves in opposition to the above views by studying what Mark actually did, not what he could or could not have done' (p. 3).

[27] On this, see F. J. Moloney, *Woman: First Among the Faithful: A New Testament Study* (Melbourne: Collins Dove, 1984) pp. 10–12.

[28] See, for this structure, R. Pesch, *Das Markusevangelium* (Herders theologischer Kommentar zum NT II/2; Herder: Freiburg, 1977) 2. Teil, pp. 345–6; K. Stock, *Boten aus dem Mit-Ihm-Sein: Das Verhältnis zwischen Jesus und den Zwölf nach Markus* (Analecta Biblica 70; Rome: Biblical Institute Press, 1975) p. 167: 'One must see in 14:17–31 a consciously constructed unit.'

was happening to Jesus, between other narratives that tell of the failure of one or all of the disciples. There is a clearly contrived pattern where the interest of the reader is shifted from the disciples (marked [A] in the structure that follows) to Jesus (marked [B]) and back to the disciples again (returning to [A]).

This deliberately contrived pattern can be seen in the following division of the passage:[29]

A]–14:1–2. Plot (*failure*).

    B]–vv. 3–9. Anointing *of Jesus*.

A]–vv. 10–11. Judas (*disciples' failure*).

    B]–vv. 12–16. *Jesus'* instructions for the Preparation of the Supper.

A]–vv. 17–21. Prediction of Judas' betrayal (*disciples' failure*).

    B]–vv. 22–25. The Supper shared by *Jesus* and *the disciples*.

A]–vv. 26–31. Prediction of the denial of Peter and the failure of all the disciples (*disciples' failure*).

    B]–vv. 32–42. The experience *of Jesus* at Gethsemane.

A]–vv. 43–52. Arrest (*disciples' failure*).

    B]–vv. 53–65. The Jewish trial of *Jesus*.

A]–vv. 66–72. Peter's denial (*disciples' failure*).

Although vv. 1–2 do not mention disciples, the need of the 'chief priests' to arrest Jesus 'by stealth' is closely linked with vv. 10–11. There Judas looks for an opportunity to betray Jesus to the 'chief priests'. Thus there is a close relationship between the discussions of the chief priests and the story of one of the disciples.

Once aware of this overall pattern, deliberately used by Mark to tell this part of his Gospel story, it is evident that we are not just dealing with a typical Marcan frame in vv. 17–31. Here there is a longer literary unit, which has as its centre the encounter between Jesus, who is going to his death, and the disciples, who (in many ways) are causing that death through their ignorance and failure. We have already seen that the story of the disciples seems to descend into deeper and more tragic failure as the Gospel progresses. Mark's telling the story of Jesus' passion in this way draws this feature of his narrative into sharp relief.[30]

Looking more closely at the section of the narrative devoted to

---

[29] I am again grateful to Michael FitzPatrick, OFM, who pointed out this structure in an unpublished paper, delivered at the Catholic Biblical Association of Australia's annual meeting in July 1988. Léon-Dufour, *Sharing*, pp. 187–8 identifies this pattern of the 'juxtaposition of light and darkness', but he takes it only as far as v. 31.

[30] The same pattern is not so clear in the second half of the Marcan passion narrative (15:1–47). This is so because the disciples are no longer playing any role in the story. In 14:50: 'They all forsook him, and fled.'

the meal, not only is the account of Jesus' meal with his disciples (vv. 22–25) framed by predictions of their ultimate failure (vv. 17–21 and vv. 26–31), but the meal is the sixth of eleven passages that have been carefully assembled by Mark. The meal has been deliberately placed in the plot as the central piece in the whole account. This overall structure indicates that the narrative is fundamentally concerned with the contrast between Jesus' gift of himself unto death and the failure of his disciples.

The Evangelist Mark is not only interested in telling a story of the passion of Jesus; he is equally concerned to tell of the failing disciples. This literary pattern is not used simply because of its 'tidiness' or because of its systematic way of presenting the details of the story. Central to the whole of Mark's presentation of the disciples is, as we have seen, a dramatic and inevitable movement on their part towards failure. This failure will reach its depths in 14:50: 'And they all forsook him, and fled.' Equally central to the Marcan story of disciples, however, is the never-failing presence of Jesus to his ever-failing disciples. Thus, while Mark 14 tells of the continued and final failure of the disciples, this story of weakness and flight is matched and finally excelled by the loving obedience of Jesus, who prays to his Father: 'Abba (Father)! Everything is possible for you. Take this cup away from me. But let it be as you, not I, would have it' (14:36; JB). Aware of this overall message, we can now turn to consider the central piece (14:17–31) of the whole account (14:1–72) in more detail.[31]

In the first section of the passage, the beginning of the frame (14:17–21), the Evangelist goes to considerable trouble to indicate that Judas, who will betray Jesus, belongs to the inner circle of his friends. We read that Jesus 'came with the twelve', a group which, as we have already seen, was especially appointed in 3:14 'to be with him' in a unique way (v. 17). The setting for Jesus' prediction of his betrayal is the meal table, another place that was sacred among friends.[32]

The tragedy is heightened by the idea that it is someone who shares table-fellowship who will betray Jesus. This theme takes us back to the role of the disciples in the feeding miracles of 6:31–44 and 8:1–10. There we saw that they wanted to 'exclude' others from the table of the Lord. Now one of them is about to break his own exclusive table-fellowship. Jesus deepens this theme further as he explains that the betrayer will be 'one who is eating with me' (v.

---

[31] See, on this, D. Senior, *The Passion of Jesus in the Gospel of Mark* (Passion Series 2; Wilmington: Michael Glazier, 1984) pp. 47–67.

[32] On the importance of 'meals' in the biblical tradition, see Léon-Dufour, *Sharing*, pp. 35–8.

18). The intimacy is intensified by the words of Jesus, which link Judas with the group of the Twelve commissioned 'to be with him' (3:14): 'It is one of the twelve, one who is dipping bread in the same dish with me.' Jesus is to be betrayed by a person who has shared the most intimate of experiences with him.[33]

A similar attention to the closeness that exists between Jesus and his future betrayers is found in the other section of the frame devoted to the rest of the disciples (14:26–31), where Jesus predicts that they 'will all fall away' (v. 27). He uses the image of the shepherd and his sheep (v. 27), but his predictions lead only to profound expressions of love and devotion. Peter swears an unfailing loyalty, better than all the others who may fall away (v. 29), and even claims that he is prepared to lay down his life out of loyalty and love for his master (v. 31). It is important to notice Mark's brief concluding remark to this passage. Peter is not alone in swearing his loyalty and love. Mark adds: 'And they all said the same' (v. 31).

There can be no mistaking Mark's desire to communicate to his readers a sense of foreboding, as these men from Jesus' most intimate circle will prove to be the very ones who betray and abandon him. Themes that began to emerge around the disciples in their failure to 'understand about the loaves, but their hearts were hardened' (6:52) have come to a head. Only now can we turn to the central piece, not only of this frame, but of the whole of 14:1–72. Shedding light on the whole of the passage we find, at its centre, the Marcan version of Jesus' last meal with these very disciples, who have not understood about the loaves, whose hearts are hardened, and who will betray and abandon him (14:22–25).

The theme of table-fellowship with the betrayers opens the passage: 'And as *they* were eating, he took bread, and blessed, and broke it, and *gave* it to *them* and said, "Take . . ."' (v. 22). This theme is continued in the sharing of the cup, where the same recipients are again specified: 'And he took the cup, and when he had given thanks *he* gave it to *them*, and *they all drank of it*' (v. 23). There is a bond between Jesus and the disciples, which Jesus does not abandon: all eat the bread broken (v. 22), all drink of the cup (v. 23) and all sing a hymn together (v. 26). Although neither Mark nor Matthew have the words 'for you' in their reporting of Jesus' words over the

---

[33] See, on this passage, V. K. Robbins, 'Last Meal: Preparation, Betrayal, and Absence', in W. Kelber (ed.), *The Passion in Mark: Studies on Mark 14–16* (Philadelphia: Fortress Press, 1976) pp. 29–34 (the whole article: pp. 21–40). Robbins's study is typical of much contemporary Marcan scholarship, which understands the disciples as completely negative characters. This approach is also marked by a 'corrective Christology'. The disciples have it completely wrong, and thus the Evangelist uses them as a foil so that he can 'correct' these errors, presumably present in the Marcan community. For a critical survey of this scholarship, see J. D. Kingsbury, *The Christology of Mark's Gospel* (Philadelphia: Fortress Press, 1983) pp. 25–45.

bread broken (as do Luke 22:19 and 1 Cor. 11:24) or the cup shared
(as does Luke 22:20), there is an intimate dialogue set up between
Jesus and the disciples around the table. He commands them, 'Take'
(14:22), and they do.[34]

However, there is more to it than the external sign of a bond
between the people around the table. The words over the bread and
the cup point to the Cross: a body given in death and blood poured
out (vv. 22, 24), but strangely they point to something beyond the
day of crucifixion. The blood is to be a covenant, 'poured out for
many' (v. 24), and Jesus comments that he will not 'drink again of
the fruit of the vine until that day when I drink it new in the
kingdom of God' (v. 25). The word 'until' rings out a message of
trust and hope that looks well beyond the events of Good Friday.

There can be no doubt that the Marcan community actually
celebrated Eucharist. This is evident from the eucharistic formulas
about eating the bread and drinking from the cup found in Mark
6:41–42; 8:7–8; 14:22–25. Similarly, Jesus' reference to the establishment of the 'kingdom of God' in 14:25 looks to another important
Marcan theme, which has been growing in importance as Jesus
moves towards his death.

In the closing section of the public ministry, in bitter polemic
with the authorities of Israel, Jesus makes his first reference to the
'new temple' founded on the rejected cornerstone (see 12:10–11).
The theme becomes more important through the Jewish trial (14:58)
and in the abuse that the passers-by hurled at the crucified Jesus
(15:29–30). In his death, the old temple is destroyed, the holy of
holies is opened through the tearing apart of the dividing veil and
made available to the whole world (15:37–38).

This 'new temple', founded on the rejected cornerstone (see
12:10), is the Marcan community itself, called to mission, and called
to a sharing of its table, where Jesus was present, no matter how
seriously the community may have failed to respond to that presence. As we have already seen in our study of the two miracles of
the multiplication of the bread, this sharing of the presence of the
Lord must take place in the mission. The disciples must feed both

---

[34] Léon-Dufour, *Sharing*, pp. 60–2, 117–18, 130–2, 195–6, rightly insists on this
'dialogic' character of the Marcan/Matthean account. What I find surprising is that,
despite his correct insistence on the importance of 'context' (see p. 183), he makes
nothing of the immediate setting of this dialogue, a passage marked by failure:
betrayal and denial.

[35] See, on this, the fine study of D. Juel, *Messiah and Temple: The Trial of Jesus in the
Gospel of Mark* (SBL Dissertation Series 31; Missoula: Scholars Press, 1977). Robbins,
'Last Meal', pp. 36–7 argues that the 'until' points beyond the Marcan community
into the parousia. For Robbins, and other scholars who share this point of view, the
Marcan community suffers from the 'absence' of Jesus, and waits, in suffering, for his
return at the parousia.

Jew and Gentile at the Table of the Lord. It is this presence that was recalled, in the midst of the disciples' failure, as they broke the bread and shared the cup in their eucharistic celebrations.[35]

This is a strange message indeed. There is to be a body given and blood poured out, which will set up a new covenant reaching beyond the Cross into the definitive establishment of the Kingdom. A covenant with whom? The readers of this passage, both the original Marcan community and all subsequent Christian communities, Jew and Gentile, are aware that the body broken and the blood poured out have indeed set up a new covenant. They form a part of that Kingdom, *thanks to the original presence of Jesus to the failing disciples*, the first recipients of the bread and the cup.[36]

> The significance of the scene is thus to be found first and foremost not in the transformation of the bread and cup or even in the meaning assigned to the bread and cup, but rather in the establishment of a community that is united to Jesus in a special way. The action over the elements is subordinate to this purpose. Through the gift which the Master symbolically makes of himself the group of twelve enters now (and will remain after the departure of Jesus) into a close contact with their host: they will be inseparable from him who is leaving them.[37]

Mark has given us an account of Jesus' gift of himself unto death so that he could set up a new and lasting kingdom with the very people who frame the narrative of the meal. The meal that Jesus shared was not a meal for the worthy ones (14:22–25). It was a meal for those people who were closest to Jesus, but who, faced with the challenge to love him even unto death, betrayed and abandoned their Lord (14:17–21, 26–31).

Conclusion

As the Marcan Church looked back over its own experience it knew, all too well, that the Lord had given himself, and that he continued to give himself to disciples who failed. This is the reason

---

[36] Robbins, 'Last Meal', pp. 21–40, misses this point, for both structural and theological reasons. He argues that the key to the interpretation of the Marcan supper is the correction of false understandings of Jesus engendered in the narrative among Pharisees, Herodians and disciples by the eating scenes of chapters 2–8. It is especially directed against those 'false prophets' who use meals to proclaim the 'presence' of Jesus (see chapters 6–8). Thus 14:12–25 is a proclamation of the suffering and crucified Jesus' 'absence' from the Marcan community. On the contrary, I am suggesting, the message is one of the 'presence' of the crucified and risen Jesus to a failing community.

[37] Léon-Dufour, *Sharing*, p. 196.

why, when they came to tell the story of the beginnings of Jesus' presence to them in the meal, they told the story in this striking way: a gift of self in love to those who have failed him most. Jesus loves his failing disciples with a love that is in no way matched by the love that they bear him.

The disciples also knew that the task of taking the Table of the Lord into the mission was not a simple one. They had to cross barriers they had never crossed before. They were summoned to share the Table of the Lord with both Jew and Gentile, but this found them wanting. Here old prejudices came to the surface. They were challenged in their moments of hesitation by the words of Jesus, which Mark reports: 'You give them something to eat' (6:36).

> The evangelist has linked Eucharistic texts with some of the most painful pastoral questions of his church: mission and reconciliation. Both involved deep divisions that may have erupted at the Eucharistic celebration; both involved painful alienations which could only be healed and ultimately reconciled in the table fellowship of Eucharist. There Jew and Gentile could share one bread; there too, a sadder-but-wiser church could repent of its failures and once again take up the bond of discipleship. The source of hope in both instances was not to be found in the fragile disciples themselves but in the compassion and strength of the Risen Christ.[38]

Mark's theology of the Eucharist is closely related to his theology of discipleship, that is, to his understanding of the Church itself. The failure of the disciples is not primarily a message on how to be a good disciple of Jesus. It is a message about the central need in the Church for a radical dependence upon the person of Jesus.

Disciples may never succeed in the response to the call to lose themselves in following the way of Jesus (see 8:34–9:1). Such a journey, which involves turning the values of the world upside-down, often produces fear and failure (see, for example, 10:52 and 16:7–8). Nevertheless, the vocation to live through the mystery of failure, depending only upon the greater mystery of the love and power of God shown to us in Jesus, stands at the heart of the message of the Gospel of Mark. It is also at the heart of the Evangelist's understanding of the eucharistic presence of Jesus to his Church.[39]

---

[38] Senior, 'Eucharist in Mark', p. 71.

[39] See Moloney, 'Vocation of the Disciples', pp. 514–15.

CHAPTER THREE

The Gospel of Matthew

The Gospel of Matthew was written some fifteen years after the Gospel of Mark. Many features of Matthew's unique story of Jesus indicate that it came to be finally produced in a largely Jewish-Christian community. This community saw that it could no longer remain within the confines of the strictly Jewish world that had formed the basic structure of earliest Christianity.

After the destruction of Jerusalem, its Temple and consequently the cult associated with the Temple in 70 CE, Israel had to reconstitute itself. Although before the Jewish War there were Sadducees, Pharisees, Essenes, Zealots and perhaps other ways of being a follower of the Law of Moses, the great survivors of the war were the Pharisees.[1] Their way of life, centred upon the Synagogue and attempting to make God relevant to every aspect of life through the Law and its application, was the basis of the Judaism that rose from the chaos of so much destruction.

The Gospel of Matthew came into existence within this historical and religious setting. It is the result of the Christian experience

---

[1] For a good study of this stage in Israel's religious and political history, see D. M. Rhoads, *Israel in Revolution 6–74 CE: A Political History Based on the Writings of Josephus* (Philadelphia: Fortress Press, 1976).

and reflection of a community that had begun its life in close association with traditional Israel. Now, in the 80s of the first century, Judaism was identified with the Synagogue. Tension and confusion were growing between Matthew's community and 'the Synagogue across the street'.[2] Ultimately, the Matthean community's belief that Jesus was the Christ forced them to move away from that old and comfortable world that they loved so much, into the Gentile mission (see especially Matt. 10:1–42; 28:16–20).

This was not an easy passage. Many members of the community wondered, worried and perhaps resisted abandoning the old and tried ways of approaching God, which they had inherited from Israel's time-honoured religion. Matthew has written a Gospel that helps the community to 'cross the bridge' from Israel into a community that bases its faith and hope in Jesus of Nazareth as the Christ, the Son of God (see Matt. 16:16).[3] This also necessarily meant involvement in the Gentile mission (28:16–20). However, both Matthew and his community seem to look back to their roots with respect. A tension between the mission to 'the lost sheep of Israel' (10:6; 15:24) and 'all nations' (28:19) is present throughout the whole of the Gospel.

Nowhere is this tension more keenly felt than in Jesus' words at the beginning of the Sermon on the Mount: 'For truly I say to you, till heaven and earth pass away, not an iota, not a dot, will pass from the law until all is accomplished. Whoever then relaxes one of the least of these commandments and teaches men so, shall be called least in the kingdom of heaven; but he who does them and teaches them shall be called great in the kingdom of heaven' (5:18–19). Jesus thus commits himself seriously to the fulfilment of the Law of Israel. However, at the end of the Gospel, the Risen Lord sends the disciples out to all nations, teaching them to observe all the things that he had taught them (28:16–20). Does this not conflict with Jesus' earlier teaching?

The answer to this important question depends upon a correct understanding of the twofold use of terms that indicate some future moment, beyond which the tiniest details of the Law would not bind. The Law would have to be lived in its perfection 'till heaven and earth pass away . . . until all is accomplished' (5:18). Just when might that time be?

---

[2] This expression comes from K. Stendahl, *The School of St Matthew* (Philadelphia: Fortress Press, 1968) 2nd ed., p. xi. Unlike many scholars, I do not think that the main thrust of the Gospel is a 'polemic' between Matthew's community and the Synagogue. The separation from the Synagogue, however, has created a crisis of identity, and confusion among Matthew's new Christians.

[3] For a presentation of the overall structure and theology of the Gospel of Matthew, see Moloney, *Living Voice*, pp. 117–43.

Perfectly coherent with his own teaching, the mission of Jesus
and also the mission of the disciples whom he sends out during his
ministry were entirely directed 'to the lost sheep of the house of
Israel' (10:6; 15:24). The two miracles that he works for Gentiles
(8:5–13, the Gentile centurion; and 15:21–28, the Canaanite
woman) are clearly given as remarkable exceptions to his rule. To
the centurion, Jesus laments the little faith of Israel, and speaks of
the future universal assembly at the table of Abraham (8:10–11) and
he responds to the woman: 'I was sent only to the lost sheep of the
house of Israel' (15:24). There is a clear intention on the part of the
Evangelist Matthew to limit the activities of the Jesus of the Gospel
story to 'the lost sheep of Israel'.

In his descriptions of the death and resurrection of Jesus, however, only Matthew records a series of events, taken from traditional
Jewish apocalyptic imagery, which mark the 'turning point of the
ages'. As Jesus dies, the Temple veil is torn from top to bottom,
there is an earthquake, rocks split, and the saints rise from their now
open tombs (27:51–54). His resurrection is marked by a further
earthquake, an angel who moves the stone, lightning and snow-
white clothing (28:2–3).[4]

Here is found the answer to the question raised by the apparent
contradiction between Jesus' teaching at the beginning of his ministry in 5:18–19 and his teaching as the Risen Lord in 28:16–20. At the
death and resurrection of Jesus, heaven and earth pass away.
Matthew understands this moment as the time when all has been
accomplished. The stage is set for a new mission: 'make disciples of
all nations' (see 28:16–20). It is, therefore, the task of the Matthean
community to accept the commission of the Risen Jesus. To cling to
'the ways of old' would mean to betray God's design for them, as it
had been revealed to them through the story of the life and teaching,
the death and the resurrection of Jesus.

Matthew's Gospel was written to convince an early Jewish-
Christian community of these truths. To write his Gospel, the
Evangelist looked to several sources for information and inspiration.
One of them (indeed his main source) was the Gospel of Mark. He
follows the order of events as they succeed one another in Mark's
Gospel, using almost all of the story of Jesus as Mark recorded it. In
addition, Matthew uses material that cannot be found in Mark, but

[4] D. Senior, *The Passion of Jesus in the Gospel of Matthew* (Passion Series 1; Wilmington:
Michael Glazier, 1985) p. 157: 'These details, most of them typical of Jewish descriptions of the endtime, give Matthew's account an electric charge and reinforce the
impression that from the moment of Jesus' obedient death a new and decisive age of
salvation has begun.'

which he seems to share with Luke,[5] and there is material that can be found only in Matthew. However, through his distinctive use of all these various 'sources' in his telling of the life and teaching of Jesus, Matthew is able to tell the story in his own way.[6] In some places he will follow the teaching of Mark, whose story he may be using, while in others he might decide to alter the Marcan perspective or tell stories of his own so that the narrative may speak more directly to his own Church on its journey away from old securities into the Gentile mission.

Disciples Who Fail

What did Matthew do with the Marcan theme of the presence of Jesus to the failing disciples in the breaking of the bread? For Mark the theme of sinfulness and failure is clearly important. It forms part of his wider theology, which makes sense of a failing discipleship. Matthew does not simply repeat Mark's message. There is a shift in his use of the theme.[7]

While in Mark the disciples will not and cannot understand the teaching and the person of Jesus, or the cost of discipleship, in Matthew they do 'understand'. In Mark, the disciples fail totally, but this is not the case in Matthew. Indeed, they often appear to grasp very clearly who Jesus is and what he is demanding of them. They fail, rather, in their inability to put into action what they have come to understand.

As in Mark, the disciples are strongly present in Matthew's versions of the two miracles of the multiplication of the loaves and the fish. Both Mark and Matthew reproduce discussions between Jesus and the disciples immediately after the miracles. We have seen that Mark points out the failure of the disciples on both occasions.[8] The Matthean parallel reinterprets this misunderstanding.

---

[5] See Introduction, note 3, on 'Q'. On this, see the fine introductory study to 'Q' by I. Havener, Q: The Sayings of Jesus (Good News Studies 19; Wilmington: Michael Glazier, 1987). For more detailed studies, see R. A. Edwards, A Theology of Q: Eschatology, Prophecy, and Wisdom (Philadelphia: Fortress Press, 1976) and the older classic by T. W. Manson, The Teaching of Jesus: Studies in Its Form and Content (Cambridge (UK): Cambridge University Press, 1935).

[6] A careful examination of Matthew's characters, plot and rhetoric would lead us to see quite a different thrust from the Marcan narrative structure. On this, see J. D. Kingsbury, Matthew as Story (Philadelphia: Fortress Press, 1986).

[7] For a good survey, see B. R. Doyle, 'Matthew's Intention as Discerned by his Structure', Revue Biblique 95 (1988) 39–41 (the whole article: pp. 34–54).

[8] See above, pp. 24–5.

Matthew does not report the disciples' *misunderstanding*. Instead, he uses a term that is often found in the Gospel of Matthew to speak of the disciples as 'men of little faith' (Greek *oligopistoi*: see 6:30; 8:26; 14:31; 16:8).

After the first feeding miracle, as Jesus comes to his frightened disciples across the sea, the reaction of the disciples is recorded as follows in Mark and Matthew:

And they were utterly astounded, for *they did not understand* about the loaves, but their hearts were hardened. (Mark 6:51b–52)	And those in the boat *worshipped him*, saying, 'Truly you are the Son of God'. (Matt. 14:33)

Mark makes it clear that matching the fear of the disciples, there was also no understanding. Matthew develops the fearfulness of the disciples. 'They were terrified, saying, "It is a ghost!" And they cried out in fear' (Matt. 14:26). Yet, despite their terror and fear they understood exactly who it was who had come to them across the waters. He is the Son of God, and they respond accordingly with an act of worship.

After the second feeding miracle, again in a boat as they cross the lake, the reaction of the disciples is recorded as follows in Mark and Matthew:

'Take heed, beware of the leaven of the Pharisees and the leaven of Herod.' And they discussed it with one another, saying, 'We have no bread.' And being aware of it, Jesus said to them, 'Why do you discuss the fact that you have no bread?' [Jesus recalls the two miracles and their aftermath.] And he said to them, '*Do you not yet understand?*' (Mark 8:14–21)	'Take heed and beware of the leaven of the Pharisees and the Sadducees.' And they discussed it among themselves saying 'We brought no bread.' But Jesus, being aware of this said, '*O men of little faith*, why do you discuss among yourselves the fact that you have no bread?' [Jesus recalls the two miracles and their aftermath.] *Then they understood* that he did not tell them to beware of the leaven of bread, but of the teaching of the Pharisees and the Sadducees. (Matt. 16:6–12)

In these two parallel passages the difference in the reaction of the disciples in their encounter with Jesus in the boat is explicit. Mark has Jesus ask the disciples 'Do you not yet understand?' (Mark 8:21), while Matthew makes the comment 'Then they understood' (Matt. 16:12). The two versions of the exchange between Jesus and his disciples that follow the accounts of the bread miracles in Mark and Matthew respectively make the differing viewpoints of each Evangelist clear. The disciples in Mark simply do not understand. This is not so with the Matthean disciples. While they *understand*, they have little faith (16:8).

The members of the Matthean community, from their own celebration of the presence of the Lord in the midst of failure, would also have sensed the truth of Mark's point of view. Mark had insisted on the never-failing presence of the Lord to his ever-failing disciples. They could appreciate this message. Even in the presence of the Risen Lord sending them out on their mission to the whole world, Matthew reports: 'And when they saw him they worshipped him; *but some doubted*' (28:17). This reflects the real-life experience of Matthew's own community, hesitating and doubting before the task of the Gentile mission.[9]

The Evangelist Matthew, strongly aware of the 'little faith' of the disciples, is nevertheless concerned to communicate a message of Jesus as the Emmanuel, God-with-us. The Gospel opens with a prophecy: 'Behold, a virgin shall conceive and bear a son, and his name shall be called Emmanuel' (which means, God with us) (1:23). Despite the little faith and the hesitation of the disciples' response to Jesus, Matthew's Gospel closes with a promise from the Risen Christ indicating that this presence will go on: 'And lo, I am with you always, to the close of the age' (28:20).

The experience of failure in Matthew's Church was different to that of the Marcan community, but the theme of the 'little faith' of the disciples makes clear that weakness and failure were a problem.[10] We have seen Mark's disciples fail increasingly as the Gospel draws to its climax, but they are not abandoned in their failure. Matthew also closes his Gospel with disciples 'doubting' before the Risen Lord himself (28:17), but this does not detract from a strong message of the presence of the Risen Christ. He writes of the Emmanuel, God in the midst of his people, until the close of the age: 'I am with you always, to the close of the age' (28:20).[11]

---

[9] For a comprehensive study, see U. Luz, 'The Disciples in the Gospel according to Matthew', in G. Stanton (ed.), *The Interpretation of Matthew* (Issues in Religion and Theology; London: SPCK, 1983) pp. 98–128.

[10] On this, see Moloney, *Living Voice*, pp. 136–43.

[11] On this, see X. Léon-Dufour, 'Présence du Seigneur Ressuscité (Mt. 20, 16–20)', in *A Cause de l'Evangile: Etudes sur les Synoptiques et les Actes offertes au Père Jacques Dupont, OSB à l'occasion de son 70e anniversaire* (Lectio Divina 123; Paris: Cerf, 1985) pp. 195–209; see especially pp. 204–9.

Israel and the Disciples at the Bread Miracles

When the Evangelist Matthew came to use the Marcan passages on the Eucharist he necessarily made changes to the basic Marcan message. Matthew's task was to communicate his message of Jesus' presence to his 'doubting' community, hesitant to leave the ways of 'the Pharisees and the Sadducees' (see 16:6, 12) to set out into the Gentile mission (see 28:16–20).[12]

From the general background of the Matthean community, it is obvious that a hesitation to leave the tried ways of the Pharisees and the Sadducees will be an important theme for the Gospel of Matthew. Written within the context of a difficult Synagogue-Christian relationship, where some of the Matthean community — challenged to embrace a Gentile mission — are sorely tempted to return to the secure ways within the Judaism that they knew and loved, Matthew saw the need to re-fashion some of the Marcan stories. This factor alters Matthew's perspective when he deals with the two bread miracles. It is evident in the following summary of this section of the Gospel of Matthew.[13]

14:13–21. *The first bread miracle.*

22–33. Jesus comes to frightened disciples on the stormy sea. Peter shows his 'little faith'.

15:1–14. Jesus attacks the traditions of Israel.

15–20. An ignorant Peter asks for an explanation of this attack.

21–28. Curing of the Canaanite woman.

29–31. Curing of many 'along the sea of Galilee', leading to the glorification of the God of Israel.

32–39. *The second bread miracle.*

16:1–4. The Pharisees ask for a sign.

5–12. Jesus and the disciples 'of little faith' discuss the leaven as they cross the lake.

13–23. Peter confesses that Jesus is the Christ, the Son of

---

[12] On the 'seeing' yet 'doubting' of 28:17 and its reflecting the Matthean community, see H. Bloem, *Die Ostererzählung des Matthäus* (Zeist: no place given, 1987) pp. 39–40. For a precise study of the Matthean community, see E. A. Laverdiere & W. G. Thompson, 'New Testament Communities in Transition', *Theological Studies* 37 (1976) 571–82 (the whole article: pp. 567–97).

[13] I am not attempting any internal structuring of this section of Matthew's Gospel. For a summary of recent attempts to do so (Gaechter, Léon-Dufour, Ellis), see J. Murphy-O'Connor, 'The Structure of Matthew XIV–XVII', *Revue Biblique* 82 (1975) 362–71. The article, which suggests an alternative structure, runs from pp. 360–84. The bread miracles do not play a crucial role in Murphy-O'Connor's suggested structure.

God and he is blessed. Jesus sets out for Jerusalem, but the same Peter refuses to accept Jesus as Son of Man and he is cursed as Satan.

As is obvious, Matthew still follows the basic Marcan story. He tells of the two miraculous feedings, but he adds to the context a more bitter attack from Jesus upon official Synagogue-centred Judaism and some severe criticism of Peter and the disciples.[14] The first miracle, the feeding of a Jewish multitude (14:13–21) leads to an encounter between Jesus, his frightened disciples and a failing Peter (vv. 22–33). Jesus then attacks Israel, but Matthew alone explains the brief 'parable' that Jesus has used concerning that which enters the mouth and that which comes out of the mouth (15:11). He responds to the disciple's concern over his treatment of the Pharisees: 'Every plant which my Father has not planted will be rooted up. Let them alone; they are blind guides. And if a blind man leads a blind man, both will fall into a pit' (15:13–14).

However, to Peter, who asked for the explanation (v. 15), he also speaks strongly: 'Are you still without understanding?' (v. 16). Matthew has prepared his readers for Peter's failure. Prior to Jesus' invective against Israel and its leaders, he has reported Peter's littleness of faith when summoned by Jesus to come to him across the stormy waters (14:28–31). Harsh though Jesus' attack upon Israel may have been, the Evangelist has no illusions about the disciples and their leader. Israel, whom Jesus has fed in the first of the bread miracles (14:13–21), may have lost its way in rejecting Jesus, but the Christian community, under the leadership of Peter, also has its moments of 'little faith' (see 14:31).[15]

The immediate aftermath of the second bread miracle is marked by two events that stress the *understanding* but the *little faith* of the disciples in general and of Peter in particular. In 16:5–12 the disciples are shown to *understand* Jesus' reference to the teaching of the Pharisees and the Sadducees (16:12), but they are still *men of little faith* (v. 8). The Evangelist then reports Peter's *understanding* that Jesus is the Christ, the Son of God (16:16). For this he receives a blessing (vv. 17–19). However, as Jesus sets out for Jerusalem, Peter fails when asked to follow a suffering Son of Man (16:22) and for this he is cursed as Satan (v. 23). Matthew alone has used terms that refer to Peter as a rock, but in contrasting ways. In 16:18 he is 'the rock'

---

[14] See Kingsbury, *Matthew as Story*, pp. 57–77.

[15] E. Schweizer, 'Matthew's Church', in Stanton (ed.), *Interpretation of Matthew*, p. 136: 'Peter says and hears *in an exemplary way for all disciples* ... This presents ... what every disciple could experience: the courage of faith which at once turns to little faith when wind and wave assail it, and which remains ultimately dependent on the gracious help of its Lord.'

(Greek *petra*) upon which the Church is built, while in 16:23 he is 'the rock of stumbling' (Greek *skandalon*).

These carefully written and strategically placed accounts of the failure of both Israel and the disciples form the context for the two bread miracles (14:13–21 and 15:32–39) at the close of Jesus' Galilean ministry. Matthew deliberately sets the two miracle stories within contexts of Jesus' increasing criticism of traditional Israel (15:1–20; 16:1–4) and failure on the part of all the disciples, and of Peter, the chief disciple (14:22–33; 15:15; 16:5–12; 21–23).[16] In 16:21 Jesus turns away from Galilee: 'From that time Jesus began to show his disciples that he must go to Jerusalem and suffer many things from the elders and the chief priests and scribes, and be killed, and on the third day be raised.'

The context of 14:13–21 makes it clear that the first multitude to be fed was Jewish. As in Mark, a study of Matthew's accounts of the two miracles again indicates that they are written in terms that recall the celebration of the Eucharist. Jesus 'took . . . looked up to heaven . . . blessed . . . broke and gave the loaves' (14:19; 15:36). Jesus' miracles of feeding with bread would have recalled the Matthean communities' own celebrations of his presence to them, nourishing them at his eucharistic table. Who are the recipients of the blessed and broken bread in the second miracle (15:32–39)?

This question needs to be asked because Matthew seems to lessen deliberately Mark's proclamation of Jesus as the one who, through his disciples, nourishes a Jewish crowd in the first miracle and Gentiles in the second. In the first miracle (14:13–21) Matthew omits all reference to the Jewish crowd as 'a sheep without a shepherd' (Mark 6:34; see Num. 27:17; Ezek. 34:5) and the sitting down in companies of hundreds and fifties (see Exod. 18:21–25; Num. 31:14; Deut. 1:15).[17] In the second miracle (15:32–39) he no longer hints at the Gentile origin of the second crowd through the

---

[16] While commentators see a close literary link between the two Marcan bread miracles, this is not the case with Matthew. See, for example, D. Patte, *The Gospel According to Matthew: A Structural Commentary on Matthew's Faith* (Philadelphia: Fortress Press, 1987) p. 223: 'Each of the two feeding stories contributes to the development of specific points and themes of the section of the Gospel to which they respectively belong.' For indications of the link between Matthew's bread stories, see the structure offered by J. Radermakers, *Au fil de l'évangile selon saint Matthieu* (Bruxelles: Institut d'Etudes Théologique, 1974) vol. 1, pp. 47–52. The two sections are entitled: 'From lack of faith to the recognition of the Son of God, by means of the bread given to the crowds' (13:53–14:36) and 'From the traditions of old to Eucharist for everyone, by means of faith in the Son of David' (15:1–39) (my translation). For Radermakers's commentary, see vol. 2, pp. 199–213.

[17] This theme is also attested at Qumran. See 1QS II, 2:21–22; CD XIII:1.

Marcan indication: 'Some of them have come a long way' (Mark 8:3).[18]

While scholars debate this question,[19] it appears to me that Matthew has made the point about Jesus as the nourisher of the Gentiles in a more subtle fashion.[20] He does it through the two episodes of the curing the Canaanite woman (15:21–28) and the curing of many people 'along the Sea of Galilee' (vv. 29–31). Although the Gentile theme is introduced through the curing of the daughter of the Canaanite woman, Matthew's message is to be found in the more briefly reported, but more spectacular, miracle 'along the Sea of Galilee . . . on the mountain' (v. 29) in 15:29–31.

He is again re-working an account that he had found in the Gospel of Mark.[21] At this stage of Jesus' ministry Mark 7:31–37 reports the cure of a deaf mute in the Decapolis, a Gentile land. Corresponding to that miracle, Matt. 15:29–31 tells of Jesus, on a mountain 'along the sea of Galilee' (v. 29), curing all who are maimed, lame, blind and dumb (v. 30; see Isaiah 35:5–6). The cure leads the unidentified crowd to respond: 'They glorified the God of Israel' (Matt. 15:31).

Matthew's miracle, administered by Jesus on the top of a mountain, forms a link between two other important 'mountain scenes' in this Gospel: 5:1–7:28 (the Sermon on the Mount) and 28:16–20 (the final commission of the Risen Jesus to his disciples). As we saw in the more general reflections on the background to the Gospel of Matthew,[22] at the beginning of Jesus' public life in the Sermon on the Mount Jesus taught that 'till heaven and earth pass away, not an iota, not a dot will pass from the law until all is accomplished' (5:18).

---

[18] It has been widely recognised that, although Matthew is using Mark, he has deliberately re-fashioned the second miracle to bring it closer to the first; he heightens the eucharistic allusions in both, and he shows more interest in the disciples and their 'little faith'. On this, see van Cangh, La Multiplication, pp. 143–8 and van Iersel, 'Die wunderbare Speisung', pp. 192–4.

[19] For the case against a Gentile audience, see van Cangh, La Multiplication, pp. 144–5.

[20] Esler, Community and Gospel, pp. 91–3, does not appreciate Matthew's subtle use of the whole context. He concludes that 'his community was composed either exclusively of Jews or exclusively of Gentiles' (p. 92).

[21] L. Cerfaux, 'La section des pains (Mc 6.31–8.26 = Matt. 14.13–16.13)', in Receuil Lucien Cerfaux (Gembloux: Duculot, 1953) vol. 1, pp. 471–85 argues against Matthew's dependence upon Mark. He suggests an original text, which pre-existed both gospels, but which already had the events in the Marcan and the Matthean sequence. See especially pp. 477–8.

[22] See above, pp. 36–9.

At the end of Jesus' ministry, as heaven and earth have passed away through the events of his death and resurrection, he sends out his disciples to 'make disciples of all nations' (28:19).

In 15:29–31, at the close of his Galilean ministry, immediately following upon his curing of the daughter of the Gentile Canaanite woman, Jesus opens the way to that final mission to the Gentiles. As the Galilean ministry began (Matt. 4:15–16), the Evangelist informed his readers that Jesus' presence in Galilee was the fulfilment of Isaiah 9:1–2:

> The land of Zebulun and the land of Naphthali,
> towards the sea across the Jordan,
> *Galilee of the Gentiles* —
> the people who sat in darkness
> have seen a great light,
> for those who sat in the region and the shadow
> of death light has dawned.

The two passages that immediately precede the second miracle of the multiplication of the bread in Matthew focus their attention upon a Gentile audience: the cure of the daughter of a Canaanite woman (15:21–28) and the curing of the multitude with many diseases (vv. 29–31). Matthew's telling his readers that, after the cure of the Canaanite woman's daughter, 'Jesus went on from there and passed *along the Sea of Galilee*' (15:29) looks back to 4:15–16 and 'Galilee of the Gentiles'. The promise of Jesus' presence to the Gentiles is now being partially fulfilled. It is only a Gentile crowd that would express its wonder by glorifying 'the God of Israel' (15:31).[23]

Perhaps Matthew means to suggest that the crowds are made up of Gentiles. He would then be following up the story of the Canaanite woman's daughter, with the apparent hesitation of Jesus to use his healing powers for the benefit of a Gentile, with this account of multiple healings of Gentiles, and the conversion of Gentile multitudes to the God of Israel. Once the barrier of racial privilege is broken at one point, the mission of Jesus no longer is restricted to Israel; among the Gentiles he heals the disabled — gives hearing to the deaf, speech to the dumb, and sight to the blind; and in the next episode he will feed the Gentiles with the bread of life as he has previously fed the thousands of Israel.[24]

---

[23] See J. C. Fenton, *Saint Matthew* (Pelican New Testament Commentaries; Harmondsworth: Penguin, 1963) p. 257; R. H. Gundry, *Matthew: A Commentary on His Literary and Theological Art* (Grand Rapids: Eerdmans, 1982) p. 319; D. Hill, *The Gospel of Matthew* (New Century Bible; London: Oliphants, 1972) p. 255.

[24] F. W. Beare, *The Gospel According to Matthew* (Oxford: Blackwell, 1981) p. 346.

The scene is thus set for the second bread miracle (vv. 32–39). Although many of the Marcan features indicating a Gentile audience may have been removed, the multitude that Jesus feeds is the crowd that has just glorified the God of Israel, 'along the Sea of Galilee'. The feeding of the immense crowd and the gathering of the seven baskets of remnants show further that the ministry to the Gentiles is not closed.[25] From 16:21 the journey to Jerusalem will begin, leading to the passing away of both heaven and earth, and the final commission to 'all nations'. The promise of Jesus' earlier contacts with the Gentile world is now part of the mission of the Church.

It appears that there is in Matthew a desire to gather Jew and Gentile, which leads this Evangelist in his report of the last moments of Jesus' Galilean ministry, to play down the contrasts between them. All are called to glorify the one God and Father of Jesus. Both the traditional leaders of Israel and the leaders of the Christian community have failed. This has been seen in the experience that Jesus had with the Pharisees (the Israel of old), all the disciples and Peter (the new Israel).[26] Yet, in the midst of so much failure, Jesus feeds both Israel (14:13–21) and the Gentiles (15:32–39). Indeed, the Gentiles come to glorify the God of Israel, as he is made known through the person and teaching of Jesus (15:31). Despite the failure of both the old and the new Israel, the mission to the Gentiles is pursued.

Thus, Matthew softens the sharp distinctions between a Jewish and a Gentile meal, but he heightens the failure of both traditional Israel under the leadership of the blind Pharisees, and the new people of God, fearful and doubting disciples under the leadership of the fearful and doubting Peter. Associating the disciples with his task, Jesus nourishes an Israel that fails (14:13–21) and a Gentile people that has glorified the God of Israel (15:31, 32–39).

The disciples collaborate in distributing the bread in both miracles (14:19; 15:36). However, Jesus gives it to them. Here Matthew makes a subtle point.[27] In reporting Jesus' giving the bread to his disciples in the first miracle (14:19), Matthew uses a tense of the Greek

---

[25] For an excellent study of Matthew 15:29–31, see T. L. Donaldson, *Jesus on the Mountain: A Study in Matthean Theology* (Journal for the Study of the New Testament Supplement Series 8; Sheffield: JSOT Press, 1985) pp. 122–35. Donaldson differs from my interpretation by concluding that Gentiles are excluded from the miracle and the meal of 15:29–39, and thus the tension between Jesus' mission to 'the lost sheep of the house of Israel' and 'all nations' is only partially resolved (see pp. 131–5).

[26] van Cangh, *La Multiplication*, pp. 145–6 shows how the theme of the *oligopistia* of the disciples is strongly present in Matthew's rewriting of Mark.

[27] I am grateful to Rod Doyle, CFC, for the suggestion that follows.

verb 'to give' indicating an action that has taken place in the past. This action of 'giving' is now closed (aorist tense *edôken*). He thus indicates that the community no longer continues simply as a Jewish community.

In the second miracle the tense of the verb 'to give' is changed. Matthew now uses a verb that indicates something that began in the past, but which continues. An action has begun that signifies the place of the Eucharist in the ongoing life of the Christian community (imperfect tense *edidou*). There is a call to be one that is unique to Matthew. Israel, Church and the Gentile world, no matter how sinful or how little their faith may be, are called to nourish and be nourished by the same Lord.[28]

Here one can trace the basic reason for Matthew's different point of view as he rewrites his Marcan source. Mark writes boldly of the radical break that must come between the newness of Christianity and the now useless ways of old. He can have Jesus proclaim: 'No one puts new wine into old wineskins; if he does the wine will burst the skins, the wine is lost and so are the skins; but new wine is for fresh skins' (Mark 2:22). Matthew does not share that point of view. The Matthean Jesus teaches: 'Neither is new wine put into old wineskins; if it is, the skins burst, and the wine is spilled, and the skins are destroyed; but new wine is put into fresh wineskins, *and so both are preserved*' (Matt. 9:17). He makes the same point when, in an almost autobiographical note, Matthew explains the task of the Christian scribe: 'Every scribe who has been trained in the kingdom of heaven is like a householder who brings out of his treasure *what is new and what is old*' (13:52).

The Marcan community had to be told the story of two miraculous feedings that recalled its eucharistic meals because of the difficulty in admitting Gentiles to its eucharistic table. It was even more urgent that these same stories be told in the Matthean community, where the struggle over the separation between Jew and Gentile was more intense and more complex. The Matthean community has grown, originally Jewish, to be increasingly Gentile, attempting to draw both, despite the sinfulness and the 'little faith' of the Christian community itself, into the one People of God around the one Table of the Lord.

---

[28] This is well summarised by Radermakers, *Au fil de l'évangile selon saint Matthieu*, vol. 2, p. 213: 'The meal table is now accessible to everyone, even the Gentiles, as long as they recognise in faith that the salvation that has been given to them comes through the people of Israel and is perfected in Jesus. The children of Israel, in their own turn, grasping the messianic significance of the cures that Jesus works, can come to the eucharistic table, that of the desert (14:13, 15) given to the twelve tribes. But it is also open to the whole of history, symbolised by the number "seven", which gathers all peoples to nourish them, through the intervention of the disciples, with bread which prevents their failing on the way' (my translation). See also pp. 206–7, where the theme of doubt and fear is dealt with.

Matthew, therefore, has no desire to alienate Israel, from which the Matthean community had come, or the Gentile mission, into which the community was now being sent. Jesus calls both Jew and Gentile into the one People of God. The Matthean community is an originally Jewish community opening itself progressively to the Gentiles. They are now together in mission to 'all the nations'. Jesus nourishes them all at the eucharistic table.[29]

The Last Supper

Matthew's account of a meal celebrated on the day before Jesus died continues as the central point of a carefully arranged scheme, which we have already traced in Mark 14:1–71. Matthew also alternates the failure of the disciples with the experience of Jesus (Matt. 26:1–75).[30] There may be elements in Matthew's Gospel that slightly soften the intensity of the Marcan critique of the disciples throughout the public ministry of Jesus, but when it comes to the passion narrative (Matt. 26:1–28:15) we find 'the damning description of their betrayal, desertion and denial'.[31] Thus, in reporting Jesus' final meal with his disciples, Matthew has no hesitation in taking up and repeating Mark's central literary pattern of betrayal — meal — betrayal (see Matt. 26:20–35).[32] Once again, the bread is broken and the wine shared as a gift of Jesus' own body and blood (26:26–29) within the setting of disciples who fail (26:20–25, Judas; 30–35, Peter and all the other disciples).

The text is almost identical to Mark 14:17–31,[33] with some slight but important variations, which actually intensify the Marcan portrait of failing disciples. In the narrative before the meal (Matt. 26:21–25) the Evangelist Matthew *heightens* the drama of Judas' betrayal. Mark has a general indication that 'one of you' (Mark 14:18), 'one of the twelve' would betray him (14:20). This indication is followed by the lament over 'that man by whom the Son of Man is betrayed' (14:21). Judas is never named, nor does he enter the story actively. The reader knows who is in question.

[29] Cerfaux, 'La section des pains', pp. 482–5.

[30] See above, pp. 29–31.

[31] Doyle, 'Matthew's Intention', p. 47.

[32] See Kingsbury, *Matthew as Story*, pp. 86–7.

[33] Commenting on the Matthean version of the supper, and its relationship to Mark's Gospel, Robbins, 'Last Meal', p. 22 comments that 'the verbal agreement indicates direct copying'. For a detailed study of Matthew's dependence upon Mark, see D. Senior, *The Passion Narrative According to Matthew: A Redactional Study* (Bibliotheca Ephemeriridum Theologicarum Lovaniensium XXXIX; Louvain: Leuven University Press, 1975) pp. 66–99.

Matthew deliberately re-fashions Mark's narrative to stress Judas' failure. Jesus first indicates generally 'one of you will betray me' (Matt. 26:21). He then shifts away from Mark's reference to one of the Twelve 'who is dipping bread in the same dish with me' (Mark 14:20) to state with specific reference to an action already completed before the eyes of all: 'He who dipped his hand in the dish with me' (Matt. 26:23). After the lament over the betrayer, which repeats almost verbatim the Marcan text, Matthew has Judas himself enter the story: 'Judas, who betrayed him, said, "Is it I, Master?" He said to him, "You have said so"' (Matt. 26:25). In Matthew, little is left to the imagination. One of the Twelve, whose name was Judas, is the betrayer. Matthew sets the scene of a clearly defined and named disciple who has shared a sacred meal with Jesus. He can now tell the Marcan story of the supper itself in an almost identical way to the Marcan version.

However, there is a feature of the Matthean account of the meal that must be noticed. Only Matthew adds to Jesus' words over the cup: 'for the forgiveness of sins' (Matt. 26:28). There is widespread agreement among scholars that Matthew has made explicit what was implicit in the other traditions: the new covenant presupposes the forgiveness of sins. All other words over the cup make reference to the covenant (see Mark 14:24; Luke 22:20; 1 Cor. 11:25), but only Matthew has words on the lips of Jesus which speak of a covenant 'for the forgiveness of sins' in a way reminiscent of Jer. 31:34 and Isaiah 53:10–12.[34]

Matthew certainly recalls the prophets' promise of a covenant for the forgiveness of sins, but is that all he does? Has Matthew's closer attention to the sinfulness of the people sharing the bread broken and the cup poured out any role to play for a better understanding of this reference to the forgiveness of sins? Matthew has repeated Mark's account of the setting and the details of the meal, but he heightens concentration upon the person of Judas, just as he will slightly increase the reader's awareness of the failure of all the disciples in the passage that follows (vv. 30–35).

Matthew's explicit reference to the blood of the covenant poured out for many *for the forgiveness of sins* (v. 28) reflects both the Matthean community's own liturgical practice, and the Evangelist's message that 'by sharing the one bread and drinking the one cup, the disciples share in the saving effects of Jesus' atoning sacrifice'.[35]

---

[34] See, for example, Léon-Dufour, *Sharing*, p. 148; Hill, *Gospel of Matthew*, p. 339; J. P. Meier, *Matthew* (New Testament Message 3; Wilmington: Michael Glazier, 1980) pp. 319–20; E. Schweizer, *The Good News According to Matthew* (London: SPCK, 1976) p. 491; Fenton, *Saint Matthew*, p. 418.

[35] Meier, *Matthew*, p. 320.

However, what is Matthew's context here? In other words, we should also ask: which disciples will share in the saving effects of Jesus' atoning sacrifice? The answer is clear: Jesus breaks his body and pours out his blood for the disciples mentioned both before and after the account of the meal itself. The forgiveness that is offered is certainly linked to the promise of the new covenant, but it is also linked to the sinfulness of the betrayers and deniers who are sharing the meal with Jesus himself.[36]

The slight alterations to the account of the future denials adds weight to this argument. Matthew has slightly retouched the Marcan account once again to make the disciples' failure more specific. While Mark has Peter claim that he would never fail Jesus, 'even though they all fall away' (Mark 14:29), Matthew has Peter indicate *why* they might fall away: 'Though they all fall away *because of you*' (Matt. 26:33). While Mark associates the rest of the disciples with Peter's profession of loyalty in general terms: 'And they all said the same' (Mark 14:31), Matthew makes specific to 'all the disciples' as he reports: 'And so said all the disciples' (Matt. 26:35).

While Matthew looks to Mark and basically repeats the account of the events of the night before Jesus died, he is able to tell it for his own Church in his own way. There was also a need in the Matthean Church to associate failing disciples with Jesus. At the eucharistic table, the members of the Matthean community recalled in their sinfulness that the founding disciples who prefigure the Matthean Church also failed. Indeed, Matthew's slight but significant reinterpretation of the Marcan version of the story focuses its attention even more closely upon the fact that it was, above all, the disciples who failed. It is to failing disciples that Jesus commands: 'Take, eat' (26:26) and 'Drink of it, all of you' (26:27).

> In the passion narrative of Mark, disciples show themselves unreliable, cowardly, betraying and denying their master. Matthew's account accentuates this. In narrative form the Evangelist is describing what is found on Jesus' lips in the fourth Gospel: 'Without me you can do nothing' (John 15:5). Up to the passion the disciples are with Jesus, or minister with his authority (10:10); in the passion they desert him, and their authority, understanding and courage desert them. Yet it is to such fallible disciples that Jesus addresses the final commission of the Gospel, and promises to be with them 'till the end of the age' (28:20b).[37]

---

[36] We have become so fascinated with the obviously important historical study of what the words and actions of Jesus at the meal meant historically (diachronically), that we lose sight of what they mean *in their present Gospel context* (synchronically).

[37] Doyle, 'Matthew's Intention', p. 47. See also pp. 51–3 on the importance of the theme of 'being-with' for Matthew's Church (i.e. 'disciples').

Conclusion

The Gospel of Matthew is not the same as the Gospel of Mark. It was written in a different place, at a different time and thus at a different stage in the history of the earliest Church. This necessarily means that it was addressed to disciples who were failing in ways different to the failures of the members of the Marcan community. As we have seen, they understand well enough, but they fall short of the total commitment required by true Christian faith. There is still doubt and hesitation when it comes to both leaving the teachings of the Pharisees and the Sadducees, and setting out into the Gentile mission.

The Gospel of Matthew also understands and presents the Eucharist as the presence of the Christ, empowering a broken people. In many ways the Matthean version of Jesus' presence to the broken at the eucharistic table is more complex. This is so because the situation he was addressing is more complex. Mark quite clearly addressed and encouraged a failing community, which had a tendency to exclude Gentiles from its eucharistic celebrations. Matthew had a more difficult task. Addressing a later generation, he is speaking to a community where both Jew and Gentile are probably being gathered at the eucharistic table.

The mission to the Gentiles, however, was not the only difficulty that the community had to face. It was not only a question of 'the new'. Matthew was also deeply concerned with 'the old'. Were the ways of old to be abandoned? Matthew objected to such a rejection of the old. Thus he had to show that both Jew and Gentile, the 'old' and the 'new' were gathered and nourished at the table of the Lord.

However, he must also show that the Church, personified in the disciples and in Peter, came to that same table to be nourished in its brokenness. No one disciple is better than the other. At the Last Supper, Matthew stresses the failure of a disciple called Judas, indeed that of the rest of the disciples along with Peter, and he insists that the blood of the covenant is poured out 'for the forgiveness of sins' (26:28). Both the Israel in which the Matthean community had its birth, but which has now been left behind, and the mission that now occupies the attention of the Matthean disciples in their own 'little faith', are being nourished at the Table of the Lord in their brokenness and need.

Despite the difference of approach that we have traced in Mark and Matthew, the theme of the presence of Jesus to a broken community is found in both gospels. Here we appear to be in touch with something that was extremely important in the understanding of the eucharistic celebrations of both the Marcan and the Matthean communities. This important and surprising approach to Christian life and practice may have belonged to the Church's 'authentic memory' of Jesus' own presence to the broken. Was it the inspiration of the lifestyle of their founder, Jesus of Nazareth, which created such an understanding of the Table of the Lord in these two communities? That is a question we must address later in this study.

We have traced the message of both Mark and Matthew through the analysis of their accounts of the multiplication of the bread and Jesus' last meal with the disciples. Although both Mark and Matthew report basically the same events, they have told them in their own way, and they have placed them in their own settings in the narratives of the gospels as a whole. We now need to look beyond Matthew and Mark to see whether the Eucharist was understood in this way by other New Testament authors, who have told these stories in a quite different fashion: Luke, John and Paul.

CHAPTER FOUR

The Gospel
of Luke

The Gospel of Luke is a remarkable work in many ways. The author is an excellent story-teller. Many of the great 'stories from the New Testament' belong to this Gospel: the Good Samaritan, Martha and Mary, the Pharisee and the Tax-collector, the Prodigal Son, Dives and Lazarus, Zacchaeus in his tree and the journey to Emmaus.

When we celebrate Christmas, it is largely the Lucan story of the annunciation, birth and infancy of Jesus that we recall. It is full of wonders as an old priest loses and then regains his speech and angels sing praise to God from on high. There is the joy of a virgin mother, the meeting of two expectant mothers, aware that their fruitfulness is a gift of God, and shepherds from the fields, summoned to the side of a newly born King of Israel. The darker shades of Matthew 1–2 hardly appear. The Wise Men from the East are the only Matthean characters to appear in our Christmas pageantry.[1]

These lasting impressions that Luke has made upon the Christian tradition over the centuries come from his great ability as a writer.[2]

---

[1] See Moloney, *Living Voice*, pp. 93–113.

[2] See the classical contribution of H. J. Cadbury, *The Making of Luke–Acts* (London: SPCK, 1927) and the more recent studies C. H. Talbert, *Reading Luke: A Literary and Theological Commentary on the Third Gospel* (New York: Crossroad, 1982) and R. C. Tannehill, *The Narrative Unity of Luke–Acts: A Literary Interpretation* (Foundations and Facets: New Testament; Philadelphia: Fortress Press, 1986).

We must not underestimate the skills of either Mark or Matthew: both have composed literary works of great power. Nevertheless, Luke outclasses them with his skills as a writer and his creative originality.

Scholars are able to look through the Gospel of Mark to identify the tradition that he received, and similarly to see how Matthew has used Mark and other sources. The task of identifying the sources for the third Gospel is not so simple. In fact, scholars still debate whether such traditional parts of the story of Jesus as his death and resurrection have been told by Luke on the basis of Mark, or whether he is telling quite a different story.[3] Nowadays, most are happy to accept that, generally speaking, Luke has Mark, 'Q' and his own traditions as sources, but he uses them very creatively.

We will encounter Luke's creativity in this study of the sections of his Gospel that are in some way eucharistic. As well as the accounts of the feeding of the multitude (Luke 9:10–17) and the Last Supper (22:14–38), Luke has added the dramatic events of the journey to Emmaus on Easter Day (24:13–35) to the Gospel traditions that speak of Jesus' presence to his disciples through the Eucharist. Luke deals with these eucharistic passages in a strikingly different fashion from Mark and Matthew. Yet, through it all, he remains faithful to the early Church's fundamental understanding of the presence of Jesus to his Church in the Eucharist.

The Multiplication of the Loaves

As we have seen, Mark and Matthew both told of two miracles in which Jesus fed the multitudes. Luke reports only one (Luke 9:10–17).[4] In both Mark and Matthew, Jesus associates the disciples closely with himself in the nourishing of the crowds through the distribution of bread. Both accounts are written to recall clearly the community's celebration of the Eucharist, especially in the description of the gestures of Jesus with the bread: taking, raising his eyes, blessing, breaking and giving. We have read the Marcan and Matthean accounts within their wider literary context. This means that we have linked together the wider 'story' by paying attention to what went before and what came after the bread miracles. We concluded that both Mark and Matthew use the bread stories to address divisions and sinfulness in their respective Churches. By

---

[3] For a critical study of this problem, see V. Taylor & O. E. Evans (ed.), *The Passion Narrative of St Luke: A Critical and Historical Investigation* (SNTS Monograph Series 19; Cambridge (UK): Cambridge University Press, 1972) pp. 3–38.

[4] Luke uses Mark 6:30–44, but very creatively. For a detailed comparison, see J. A. Fitzmyer, *The Gospel According to Luke I–IX* (Anchor Bible 28; New York: Doubleday, 1981) pp. 762–3. See also Cerfaux, 'La section des pains', p. 481, note 1.

looking back upon the failures from the story of Jesus, the Evangelists are able to address the sinfulness of their own communities. In each case they use the presence of the eucharistic Jesus to disciples to exhort and encourage failing disciples, both in the 'then' of the story of Jesus and in the 'now' of the Christian community.[5]

The Lucan version of this event makes quite a different point. It comes at a stage in Luke's narrative where the Evangelist has deliberately eliminated a large section of the Marcan story. Luke does not report Mark 6:44–8:27. Scholars generally refer to this feature of the Gospel of Luke as 'the great omission'. It was within that section of the Gospel of Mark (repeated in the Gospel of Matthew) that the contrast and conflict between Jesus and Israel developed, and where Jesus moved from Israel into the Gentile world, challenging hesitant disciples to do the same. In our study of the two bread stories in both Mark and Matthew it was precisely this 'great omission' that provided the wider context for the miracles. This does not take place in the Gospel of Luke.

One of the important themes in both the Gospel of Luke and the Acts of the Apostles is the founding significance of the Apostles. Luke's two volumes were written in a Gentile world for Christians who were wondering about their origins. Far flung from the 'beginnings' of the Christian movement, they needed to be told clearly that they belonged firmly to those beginnings. One of Luke's methods for doing this is to associate the disciples very closely with Jesus throughout his ministry. Indeed, across the whole of Luke–Acts they are deliberately presented by Luke as repeating the experiences of Jesus in their own Christian lives.[6]

These disciples were the 'apostles' eventually responsible for bringing the person and teaching of Jesus Christ to all the nations (see Luke 24:46–47; Acts 1:8).[7] Although the term 'apostle' had already been used in its Christian sense by Paul (see, for example, Rom. 1:1; 11:13; 1 Cor. 1:1; 15:9; Gal. 1:17, 19, etc.), it becomes most important for Luke (see Luke 6:13). The noun, from the Greek verb *apostellein* meaning 'to send out', is applied to the Twelve Apostles, the original missionaries who form the foundation of the post-Easter Church (see 6:13). They were the link between the Church of

---

[5] See above, pp. 34–5 and 52–3.

[6] On this, see R. F. O'Toole, *The Unity of Luke's Theology: An Analysis of Luke–Acts* (Good News Studies 9; Wilmington: Michael Glazier, 1984) pp. 62–94.

[7] For a more detailed presentation of this theme, see Moloney, *Living Voice*, pp. 67–92.

the time of Luke and the time of Jesus himself (see, for example, Luke 24:33–34; Acts 1:15–26).[8]

Luke 9:1–51 can be understood in the light of the crucial role of the 'apostles'. Here they receive important instruction concerning both the person of Jesus and their own destiny before they set out with Jesus on the road to Jerusalem (9:51). The chapter opens with instructions of the Twelve for mission. They are then sent out (Luke 9:1–6; see also Mark 6:6b–13). While they are away, the Herod episode, which had been told in such detail in Mark (Mark 6:14–29), is reduced to a minimum (Luke 9:7–9). Luke focuses the reader's attention on Herod's question about the person of Jesus. Herod asks: 'Who is this about whom I hear such things?' (v. 9). The apostles return, and the bread miracle follows (vv. 10–17).[9] A part of the answer to Herod's question has been answered: he is a worker of great signs, able to nourish the multitudes, but there is more to it.

As was the case in the gospels of Mark and Matthew, the disciples are associated with the nourishing of the multitudes. There is an important difference in detail, however. While in both Mark and Matthew they are called 'the disciples' (Mark 6:35; Matt. 14:15), in Luke they are called 'the twelve' (Luke 9:12). The 'twelve' ask Jesus to send the people away (v. 12), but he commands them: 'You give them something to eat' (v. 13). However, it is Jesus who takes from their poverty (five loaves and two fish), looks up to heaven, blesses, breaks, 'and gave them to the disciples to set before the crowd' (v. 16). After the feeding, with its obvious eucharistic overtones, twelve baskets remain. As J. A. Fitzmyer has commented: 'The "twelve" baskets obviously has a symbolic reference to the "Twelve" in v. 12; they each bring back a basketful and now have enough to feed still others.'[10] Luke's vision of founding apostles is very important in his re-telling of the traditional story of the feeding of the multitudes. The association of 'the twelve' in the story of Jesus *then*, makes sense of a Church looking back to trace its own roots in the life of Jesus to make sense of its *now*.[11]

---

[8] For a survey of the very complex discussion over the development of the concept and language of an 'apostle' in the early Church, see D. Müller & C. Brown, article 'Apostle' in C. Brown (ed.), *The New International Dictionary of New Testament Theology* (Exeter: Paternoster Press, 1975) vol. 1, pp. 128–37.

[9] It is here that the 'great omission' of Mark 6:44–8:27 occurs.

[10] Fitzmyer, *Luke I–IX*, p. 769.

[11] See van Cangh, *La Multiplication*, pp. 148–55; van Iersel, 'Die wunderbare Speisung', pp. 148–55.

Further answers to Herod's question are now provided by Peter's confession that Jesus is 'the Christ of God' (v. 20), complemented by the voice from heaven announcing that Jesus, who converses with the lawgiver, Moses, and the founding prophet, Elijah, is also 'my Son, my Chosen' (v. 35). Again, some of the apostles, Peter, James and John, witness this (vv. 28, 32–33). Driving out the demon that was beyond the authority of the disciples leads to dismay and 'all were astonished at the majesty of God' (vv. 37–43). This series of revelations that respond to the question posed by Herod comes to a conclusion when Jesus solemnly announces to the disciples: 'Let these words sink into your ears; for the Son of Man is to be delivered into the hands of men' (v. 44).

As throughout the Synoptic tradition, titles of honour and indications of the ultimate authority of Jesus do not tell the whole story. There is always a clear indication that such honour and authority come only through the experience of the Cross. It is not enough to 'marvel at everything' (v. 43b). The disciples must be profoundly aware that they are following Jesus to suffering and death in Jerusalem. It is this awareness that is demanded from them by the words of Jesus that only Luke reports: 'Let these words sink into your ears' (v. 44).

There is a deliberate association of the disciples with Jesus throughout the gradual revelation of Jesus' person, dignity . . . and destiny. As well as being the recipients of this revelation, threaded through the whole of the narrative one finds explicit instructions to the disciples (see vv. 1–6, 23–27, 46–50). Climaxing the first half of the Gospel and opening the second, the Evangelist announces: 'When the days drew near for him to be received up, he set his face to go to Jerusalem. And he sent messengers ahead of him' (v. 51). The future founding apostles of the Churches have now been instructed on their task, and they have been shown who it is they are following. They now set out for Jerusalem *together*.

This overview of Luke 9:1–51 shows that the themes that were developed by the respective Evangelists around both the Marcan and the Matthean bread miracles are not found in Luke. It was important, for the purposes of our study, to show how each Evangelist uses this eucharistic material. Luke's closing section of the Galilean ministry (9:1–50) is highlighted by the instruction of the future twelve apostles. But there are three further significant meals in the Gospel: the meal shared by Jesus and the apostles on the day of the Unleavened Bread (22:7, 14–38), a meal that Jesus shares at Emmaus with two of his disciples (24:13–35), and a final meal with 'the eleven' who have remained in Jerusalem (24:36–49). Luke will tell of these meals to show that apostles and disciples did

not always live up to the instructions they received in those days
before they set out for Jerusalem (9:1–50).

The Last Supper

Luke presents an account of the disciples' last meal with Jesus
(22:14–38) that is strikingly different from that of Mark and Matthew. Indeed, he was probably not depending upon Mark for this
part of his story, but drew it from other sources.[12] Rather than
concentrate on Luke's use of possible sources, recent studies have
tended to look to this narrative as a fine example of Luke's literary
skills.

Two themes in particular seem to be intertwined in this account.
Throughout the whole of the Gospel of Luke there is a notable
interest in food and meals.[13] This theme comes to a climax in the
final meal celebrated with the twelve before Jesus dies (22:14–38),
and in the meal that the Risen Lord shares with those same apostles,
less Judas (24:36–49). A further feature of the Lucan Last Supper is
its setting within a long 'final discourse' that Jesus delivers to his
disciples.[14]

The Lucan Meals and the Last Meal

The supper that is recorded in 22:14–38 is part of a long series of
suppers through the Gospel. These suppers are consistently marked
by Jesus' questioning the status quo. He shares the table with
sinners, he radically questions the Pharisees on the numerous occasions where he is reported to have been invited to dine with them.[15]

Jesus shared a meal with Levi, the sinful tax-collector. More than
that, there were other sinners at the table who had been gathered by
Levi to share fellowship with Jesus (5:27–32). Invited as 'a prophet'
(see 7:39) to share the table with another important religious figure,
Simon the Pharisee, Jesus shows that his love cannot be contained
within the limitations of conventional religion. He allows and even
encourages the intimacy of a woman well known for her sins (7:37).

---

[12] For a detailed analysis, see J. A. Fitzmyer, *The Gospel According to Luke X–XXIV*
(Anchor Bible 28A; New York: Doubleday, 1985) pp. 1385–406.

[13] See the study of R. J. Karris, *Luke: Artist and Theologian: Luke's Passion Account as
Literature* (New York: Paulist Press, 1985) pp. 47–78. See also J. Neyrey, *The Passion
According to Luke: A Redaction Study of Luke's Soteriology* (New York: Paulist Press, 1985)
pp. 8–11; M. Barth, *Rediscovering the Lord's Supper*, pp. 71–4.

[14] See especially Léon-Dufour, *Sharing*, pp. 85–95, 230–47; Neyrey, *Passion According
to Luke*, pp. 5–48.

[15] For a detailed study of the significance of sharing one's table in Jewish thought and
practice, see Esler, *Community and Gospel*, pp. 71–86.

Her love has drawn her to the table and to Jesus' forgiveness (7:36–50). Again at table with the Pharisees, he challenges them to recognise their lack of true justice (11:37–54). He uses a further meal with the Pharisees to heal the disadvantaged man with dropsy on a Sabbath, to question the way the Pharisees 'religiously' organised their meals, and to urge them to follow his example: 'When you give a feast, invite the poor, the maimed, the lame, the blind, and you will be blessed because they cannot repay you' (14:14, see 14:1–24).

The challenge that Jesus issues through the sharing of meals and his questioning of the status quo within the context of these meals is important for Luke. He is also looking to the *then* of the life of Jesus to question the *now* of current Christian practice. Commenting on Luke's parable of the great supper (14:16–24), J. R. Donahue concludes:

> Within Christian communities, some of the most violent debates continue to rage over inclusiveness, often centred on the celebration of the Lord's Supper. Yet when Luke's Jesus told a parable about eating bread in the kingdom of God, he shattered his hearer's expectations of who would be the proper table companions. Can his parabolic word continue to challenge our expectations?[16]

The final eloquent witness to this important Lucan theme is found in 19:1–10. As Jesus approaches Jerusalem, he catches sight of Zacchaeus. Despite the murmuring opposition of the people standing by, Jesus publicly announces that he will stay and dine with Zacchaeus, a chief tax-collector. In his own turn, Zacchaeus commits himself to the way of Jesus by promising to give half his possessions to the poor.

Jerome Neyrey has commented on Luke's use of Jesus' shared meals:

> Jesus' inclusive table fellowship mirrors the inclusive character of the Lukan Church: Gentiles, prostitutes, tax collectors, sinners, as well as the blind, lame, maimed and the poor are welcome at his table and in his covenant.[17]

Luke has no illusions about the composition of his Church. It is not made up of a group of 'perfect people'. On the contrary, it is made up of people who have become Christians because they have been

---

[16] J. R. Donahue, *The Gospel in Parable* (Philadelphia: Fortress Press, 1988) p. 146.

[17] Neyrey, *Passion According to Luke*, p. 10. See the excellent synthesis of Kodell, *Eucharist*, pp. 106–13. See also J. Massyngbaerde Ford, *Bonded with the Immortal: A Pastoral Introduction to the New Testament* (Wilmington: Michael Glazier, 1987) pp. 280–9.

the recipients of the witnessing of the apostles. The Risen Christ commissions his apostles:

> Thus it is written that the Christ should suffer and on the third day rise from the dead, and that repentance and forgiveness of sins should be preached in his name to all nations, beginning from Jerusalem. You are witnesses of these things. And behold I send the promise of my Father upon you; but stay in the city until you are clothed with power from on high. (24:46–49; see also Acts 1:8)

It is from this background of meals shared with sinners that we can best understand 22:14: 'And when the hour came, he sat at table and the apostles with him.'[18] Despite the importance for the overall argument of Luke–Acts that the apostles must play an essential and foundational role 'on the other side' of the death and resurrection of Jesus, Luke wants to show that they too share this final meal with their Master as sinners and broken people. They are the last of a long group of broken and sinful people who have shared meals with Jesus during his life and ministry.

Luke's understanding of 'the broken' who gather at the Table of the Lord is broader than that of Mark and Matthew. No longer is it simply a question of Gentile and Jew sharing a table founded upon disciples who had failed Jesus. For Luke there are many ways in which one can be considered an outsider. There are those who are guilty of sin, such as the prostitute and the tax-collector, and there are Pharisees who suffer from their self-righteousness. There are disciples who fail Jesus, through the weakness of their faith, and there are members of the Twelve who deny him (Peter) and who betray him (Judas). Finally, there are the Gentiles and the physically maimed people from the highways and the byways who are all welcomed at the table of Jesus.

Within this broad canvas of broken people who are offered the possibility of a real salvation through sharing meals with Jesus, the apostles will be able to give eloquent witness to repentance and forgiveness of sins to all the nations (24:47). Their own lives as followers and apostles of Jesus result from such an experience. They experience the repentance and forgiveness to which they eventually bear witness. As Philip Esler has recently shown, Jesus' practice of sharing meals with outcasts will be continued by the apostles themselves in Luke's second volume, the Acts of the Apostles. While the theme of Jesus' acceptance and forgiveness of the broken highlights his table in the Gospel, the early Church's acceptance of

---

[18] Only Luke writes 'and *the apostles* with him'. Compare Mark 14:17: 'He came with the twelve' and Matt. 26:20: 'He sat at table with the twelve disciples'.

the Gentiles marks the tables shared by the apostles in the Acts of the Apostles. Commenting on the conversion of Cornelius in Acts 10:1–11:18, Esler comments: 'What matters to Luke is the legitimation of complete fellowship between Jew and Gentile in the Christian community, not just the admission of the Gentiles to those communities.'[19] Apostles who have experienced forgiveness and admission to the table of the Lord are able to preach and practice such a mission to further 'outsiders'.

The theme of Jesus' presence to the broken and the sinful throughout the whole Gospel, which stands at the basis of what the apostles will witness to the ends of the earth, reaches its high point at the Last Supper. 'This final meal on the feast of Passover crowns the meals, both everyday and festive, which he has taken with his disciples and with sinners during his earthly life.'[20]

The theme of meals celebrated by Jesus is continued into the Last Meal. We have already seen that Mark used a pattern of alternating the actions of Jesus and the failure of the disciples in Mark 14:1–71.[21] There he told the story of the last moments of Jesus' unfailing presence with his failing disciples. It is quite possible that Luke was using his version of a similar alternating pattern in his construction of Luke 22:14–38.

Luke's account of the Last Supper alternates between Jesus' teaching about the establishment of the Kingdom through his death and resurrection, and the apostles' involvement in it on the one hand, and explicit indications of the future betrayal and denial of these same apostles on the other. The passage can be presented as follows:

A] vv. 14–18. The sharing of the first cup, and the promise of the fulfilment of the Kingdom.

    B] vv. 19–23. The account of the meal and the prediction of the betrayal of Judas.[22]

A] vv. 24–30. The part that the disciples will play in the Kingdom.

    B] vv. 31–34. The prayer of Jesus for Peter, but the prophecy that he will yet deny Jesus.

---

[19] Esler, *Community and Gospel*, p. 96. His excellent study of the sharing of the table in Acts is found on pp. 93–109. Unfortunately he has not considered the theme in Luke's Gospel at all.

[20] Léon-Dufour, *Sharing*, p. 233.

[21] See above, pp. 29–31.

[22] There is difficulty with the original text here, as some ancient manuscripts omit the second word over the cup. In defence of the longer reading, see Jeremias, *Eucharistic Words*, pp. 139–59. For a briefer survey, see Fitzmyer, *Luke X–XXIV*, pp. 1387–9. Even if one were to accept the shorter reading (which I do not), my structure would still hold.

A] vv. 35–48. The difficulties that will confront the disciples in their future mission.

There are, however, many differences between the Marcan and the Lucan schemes. While the alternation of themes is present, the literary form in Luke 22:14–38 is a final discourse. Jesus is speaking throughout. In Mark 14:1–71 we found the blending of direct speech and narrative. Unlike Mark, it is not only in those sections explicitly dedicated to betrayal and denial (vv. 19–23 and 31–34) that Luke develops the theme of the failure of the apostles. It is all-pervading.

Here we can sense the hand of a skilful author. The sinners are strongly present. We read in v. 21 that 'the hand of him who betrays me is with me on the table'. The obtuseness and brokenness of the apostles in general are indicated through the report of a dispute in v. 24. Peter's betrayal is predicted v. 34. It is reported that the apostles will need 'strengthening' (v. 32), implying that they are weak and frail. They seem, moreover, to misunderstand Jesus' missionary instructions in vv. 35–38. While Jesus hints of the trials, imprisonments, persecutions and death that await the apostolic mission, and which indeed take place in the Acts of the Apostles, they take his symbol of a 'sword' literally. This leads to Jesus' comment to close all such discussion: 'Enough!'[23] T. W. Manson has described this final reaction of Jesus to his failing disciples as 'the utterance of a broken heart'.[24]

Jesus' table includes Judas (his betrayer), Peter (who denied him) and the squabbling and obtuse apostles. Jesus eats with people who fail, even at the Last Supper. Although handled with more subtlety than Mark or Matthew, the presence of Jesus to his disciples at the Last Supper is a presence to the broken. Luke has drawn this theme, which has marked so many of the meal scenes throughout the Gospel, to a fitting conclusion in 22:14–38. They will be worthy candidates for the future mission, witnessing to repentance and the forgiveness of sins to all the nations (24:47).[25]

The motley group that shares the table of the Lord, and which indicates how this table should be administered in the Church has been well described by Markus Barth:

---

[23] For an excellent commentary upon Luke 22:35–38, which I have followed, see Neyrey, *Passion According to Luke*, pp. 37–43. Along the same lines, see Fitzmyer, *Luke X–XXIV*, pp. 1428–31.

[24] T. W. Manson, *The Sayings of Jesus* (London: SCM Press, 1971) p. 341. See also P. S. Minear, 'A Note on Luke 22:36', *Novum Testamentum* 7 (1964–65) 128–34.

[25] See Léon-Dufour, *Sharing*, p. 234.

Whoever sits at table with Jesus must also accept the other guests in Christ's company. Jesus is never without his elect, including especially the outcast. No one can have Jesus for oneself alone; Jesus is met with a strange entourage — the publicans and the sinners, the poor and the bums from the hedges and byways, a notorious woman whom Jesus permitted to touch his feet, the prodigal sons and such treacherous and cowardly disciples as Judas and Peter and the other disciples who partook of Jesus' last meal (none of whom loved him enough to arrange his funeral). Whoever considers those table companions of Jesus too bad, too base, too little, too far removed from salvation to be met at Jesus' side does not see, accept, and believe Jesus as he really is. Whoever feels too good and too noble to be found in that company cannot sit at the Lord's table. Only when the bums just mentioned have been received and waited upon is Jesus received, and only then does Jesus accept the service rendered to him.[26]

A Meal that is also a Farewell Discourse

The other important feature of Luke 22:14–38 that has been noticed by recent scholarship is Luke's use of a 'farewell speech' technique. We have already seen that the structured presentation of the text above[27] differs from Mark's similar use of a pattern of alternating themes. This is due, largely, to the fact that Luke's report of the Last Supper is not only a narrative about a shared meal but also a final discourse. There is a quite different point of view being expressed.

In Mark 14:1–71 the account of Jesus' words and actions with the bread and wine at the supper formed the very centrepiece of the whole passage. This is not the case with Luke. Indeed, it is only a part of the second section of the structure (22:19–23), dedicated to the prophecy of the betrayal of Judas. Luke 22:14–38 is not primarily about Jesus' eucharistic words. It is about the last testimony that Jesus left his disciples, within the context of a meal, as he parted from them. As Paul Minear has rightly commented, 'In this story the center of gravity lies not in the words of institution but, as at earlier tables, in the four key dialogues between Jesus and the disciples.'[28]

The practice of placing a 'farewell speech' on the lips of a great man as he goes to his death is a reasonably common practice in

---

[26] Barth, *Rediscovering the Lord's Supper*, p.73. See also Kodell, *Eucharist*, p.105: 'The Last Supper is the final meal in a series during Jesus' ministry. There he teaches his disciples how they are to act after he is gone by his interpretation of the bread and wine, by his last instructions, and by sharing table fellowship with his betrayer.'

[27] See above, pp.62–3.

[28] P. S. Minear, 'Some Glimpses of Luke's Sacramental Theology', *Worship* 44 (1970) 326 (the whole article: pp.322–31).

many religious writings from the first three centuries of the Christian era.[29] It is particularly widespread in the biblical literature.[30] In the Old Testament we find farewell speeches in Genesis 47–50 (Jacob), in Joshua 23–24 (Joshua) and in Deuteronomy 31–34 (Moses). In the New Testament, Jesus (John 13–17; Luke 22:14–38), Peter (2 Peter 1:12–15) and Paul (Acts 20:17–35), each give a farewell speech. There is now considerable interest on the part of New Testament scholars in a series of other Jewish testamentary texts where this technique is used, especially *The Testaments of the Twelve Patriarchs*, written in the second century BCE, modelled on Jacob's last words in Genesis 49.[31]

From the following outline of the main features of a farewell speech, it will be noticed that Luke 22:14–38 is an excellent example of this genre.[32] There are four basic elements to this form.

1. *Prediction of death*. The speech is understood by the patriarch who is about to depart as his 'farewell' to his disciples. Thus there is some indication or prediction of his oncoming death in all of the testaments. In some cases, the death is unexpected (*Testament of Levi* 1:2; *Testament of Naphtali* 1:2–4; *Testament of Asher* 1:2). This prediction serves as the occasion for the speech. In Luke's Last Supper discourse, this is found in 22:15: 'I have earnestly desired to eat this passover with you before I suffer', and again in 22:22: 'For the Son of Man goes as it has been determined.'

2. *Predictions of future attacks upon the dying leader's disciples*. This feature of the farewell speech is also basic to its structure. One of the motivations for the speech is to forewarn disciples that they are in imminent danger. Most of the testaments portray this imminent danger as a sign of the endtime. In the Lucan text this feature is found in 22:31–34: 'I have prayed for you that your faith may not fail; and when you have turned again, strengthen your brethren . . . I tell you, Peter, the cock will not crow this day, until you three times deny that you know me.' It is also present in 22:36: 'Now let him who has a purse take it, and likewise a bag. And let him who has no sword sell his mantle and buy one.'

---

[29] For a discussion, see C. H. Dodd, *The Interpretation of the Fourth Gospel* (Cambridge (UK): Cambridge University Press, 1953) pp. 420–3.

[30] For what follows I am depending on the work of Neyrey, *Passion According to Luke*, pp. 6–8.

[31] For an introduction and an annotated critical text of this document (prepared by H. C. Kee), see J. H. Charlesworth (ed.), *The Old Testament Pseudepigrapha* (London: Darton, Longman & Todd, 1983) vol. 1, pp. 775–828.

[32] Here I am following the results of the research of Neyrey, *Passion According to Luke*, p. 7. See also Léon-Dufour, *Sharing*, pp. 245–6.

3. *There is an exhortation to ideal behaviour.* The testaments devote a lot of attention to the difficulties to be endured in the future. They are to be met with a behaviour that will both protect the members of the group from danger, and help them to overcome their difficulties. Here there is a slight intrusion of the uniquely Lucan use of his meal theme, where failing disciples are the object of his exhortation. The instruction to ideal behaviour of the 'farewell discourse' is found within the context of disciples who squabble (22:24).[33] The exhortation then follows in vv. 25–26:

> The kings of the Gentiles exercise lordship over them; and those in authority over them are called benefactors. But not so with you; rather let the greatest among you become as the youngest, and the leader as one who serves (see the whole of vv. 24–27).

4. *The final commission.* There are instructions given to the disciples of the departing patriarch concerning their reconstitution after his departure. Again the fact that Luke has blended his theme of Jesus' presence to the broken at the meal table intrudes slightly, as it is within the context of a future denial that Peter is commissioned (vv. 33–34). Nevertheless, even though the commission is delivered to failing disciples, it still stands. The apostles are to continue what he has left with them, even after his departure. This is found in Luke 22:31–32: 'Simon, Simon, behold Satan demanded to have you that he might sift you like wheat, but I have prayed for you that your faith may not fail; and when you have turned again, strengthen your brethren.'[34]

The use of the theme of the meal has served Luke to show that Jesus shared his Last Supper with broken disciples, while his use of the literary form of a farewell discourse establishes them as his legitimate successors. Both themes are important for Luke. His skilful writing has enabled him to blend both the meal theme and

---

[33] In the testaments there are frequent references to the *future* failings of the patriarchs' sons, generally associated with the endtime. See, for example, *Testament of Levi* 10:1–5; 14–16; *Testament of Isacchar* 6:1–4; *Testament of Dan* 5:7–8; *Testament of Naphtali* 4:1–5. On one occasion only there is a reference to present sinfulness, but the patriarch's exhortation quickly moves into a discussion of the evils of the endtime. See *Testament of Judah* 23:1.

[34] Neyrey, *Passion According to Luke*, pp. 31–7 offers an excellent study of these verses. He shows convincingly that Jesus' words are a 'commissioning' of Peter. He even suggests 'that this verse (32b) contains a solemn commissioning of Peter comparable to Mt. 16:17–19 and Jn 21:15–17' (p. 34). The theme of failure on the part of the commissioned future leader is also an important result of Luke's 'blending' of his meal theme with the 'farewell discourse'. See, on this, Léon-Dufour, *Sharing*, pp. 241–2, although he does not identify the 'blending' as producing this theme.

the pattern of a farewell speech.[35] This blending has not been purely for aesthetic reasons. By intermingling both, he has been able to continue the tradition, found in both Mark and Matthew, of the presence of Jesus to the broken and sinful disciples.

We have seen that Luke's skilful blending of meal and farewell discourse produces a rather unique form of the 'farewell discourse', where disciples are instructed and commissioned in the midst of failure. One is not sharply aware of this tension in the narrative, even though it does produce a rather singular example of the 'farewell discourse' form. Luke has written 22:14–34 with great skill, showing that these very disciples, despite the brokenness of their table-fellowship with the Lord, are also the apostles, the ones who will continue his presence 'to all nations' (24:47; Acts 1:8).[36]

A departing Jesus commissions failing disciples in a farewell discourse delivered at the last of a long series of meals that Jesus has shared with broken people. The message is clear:

> Jesus will not distance himself from them because they fail him. The keynote of his ministry, and especially his table fellowship has been 'He was reckoned with transgressors' (Is. 53:12; Lk. 22:37), both by his own desire and the will of his persecutors (see 23:32). And he will continue to share his life with sinners in the kingdom meals of the time of the Church.[37]

The Journey to Emmaus

Mark and Matthew both promise the reconstitution of a disbanded and failed group of disciples 'on the other side' of Jesus' death and resurrection. They both do this within the context of the Last Supper: 'I shall not drink again of the fruit of the vine, *until that day* when I drink it new in the kingdom of God' (Mark 14:25; see Matt. 26:29). Neither Mark nor Matthew report that after the resurrection

---

[35] This 'blending' of the themes of failure and commissioning for a future brings its difficulties. The patriarch never gives his instructions to the sort of squabbling disciples found in Luke 22:24–27. Although the testaments do speak of a future sinfulness, the 'commissioning' never takes place within the context of a prophecy of future denial of the patriarch. See, on this, Léon-Dufour, *Sharing*, pp. 236–9 and 243–5. He notes that 'certain departures from the testamentary genre are significant' (pp. 243–4). I am suggesting that they arise largely from Luke's blending of his meal theme with the testamentary genre.

[36] Here we find another marked difference between the *Testaments of the Twelve Patriarchs* and Luke 22:14–38. Many of the patriarchs speak at length of their sinful past, especially their sexual dalliances and their mistreatment of Joseph. See, for example, *Testament of Reuben* 1:6–10; 2:11–15; *Testament of Simon* 2:6–13; *Testament of Gad* 2:1–5. Obviously, there is no place for this theme in the Gospel.

[37] Kodell, *Eucharist*, p. 117.

this promise is fulfilled. It was not needed, as the prophecy points to the actual celebration of the Eucharist as it was practised in both the Marcan and the Matthean communities.

Luke maintains this tension, which looks to a later moment when Jesus will again celebrate a meal with his disciples. Indeed, he has Jesus make such a prediction twice (Luke 22:16 and 18). Luke, however, goes further than either Mark or Matthew by reporting two occasions when the Risen Jesus actually shares a meal with his disciples. The first of these meal scenes is recorded in Luke 24:13–35: the journey to Emmaus.

Luke links all the episodes of his resurrection account by insisting that everything took place on the one day. He opens his account by naming that day: 'On the first day of the week' (24:1). We are next told, 'That very same day two of them were going to a village named Emmaus' (v. 13). Towards the end of their journey we read, 'Stay with us for it is towards evening and the day is now far spent' (v. 29). After the breaking of the bread, 'They rose that same hour and returned to Jerusalem'. They make their report, but 'as they were saying this, Jesus himself stood among them' (v. 36). This is the final presence of Jesus to his disciples in the Gospel (see v. 51, where he leaves them).

For Luke, the whole of his Gospel has been directed towards this 'day'. As he began his journey towards Jerusalem in 9:51, the Evangelist commented, 'When the days drew near for him to be received up, he set his face to go to Jerusalem'. That 'journey' comes to its close in Jerusalem through 'the things that have happened there' (24:18). On this resurrection 'day' we sense that we are at the end of a long journey.

In fact, one of the most important themes of the Gospel of Luke and its companion work, the Acts of the Apostles, is the theme of a journey.[38] Throughout the Gospel, a journey leads to Jerusalem, where the paschal events take place (see especially 9:51). At the beginning of Acts, the early Church is still in Jerusalem. The Spirit is given there, and it is from there that a second journey begins, reaching out to the ends of the earth. The centre-point of Luke–Acts is the city of Jerusalem. The journey of Jesus leads him there. In Jerusalem the paschal events take place, and he ascends to his Father from that city. Jerusalem is the end of the journey of Jesus. The journey of the apostles begins there. They are commissioned to go out to all the nations, but they are to 'stay in the city' to await the gift of the Spirit (24:49). There they are given the Spirit (Acts 2:1–13), there they first become 'Church', one in heart and soul, celebrating the Lord's presence in their meals (2:42–47). However, it

---

[38] On this theme through the Gospel of Luke, see Moloney, *Living Voice*, pp. 67–92.

is from there that they eventually set out, witnesses 'in Judea and Samaria and to the ends of the earth' (Acts 1:8; see also 20:7–11; 27:33–36).[39] The city of Jerusalem acts as a fulcrum, around which God's salvation history swivels.[40]

This theme is important for a correct understanding of Luke's story of the journey to Emmaus. If Jerusalem is the centre of God's history, and if the whole of Luke's resurrection account centres its attention upon the 'day' on which Jesus' journey comes to an end in Jerusalem, then the opening remarks of the journey to Emmaus are an indication of the situation of the two disciples. We are told that in the midst of the paschal events they were going to Emmaus, 'about sixty stadia *away from Jerusalem*' (24:13).[41] They are walking away from Jerusalem, the central point of God's story; away from God's journey from Nazareth to the ends of the earth!

This impression is further reinforced once one begins to notice the details of the account itself. In their sadness and disappointment the disciples do not recognise Jesus (v. 15–17). They tell him of their expectations: 'We had hoped that he was the one to redeem Israel' (v. 21). Jesus' way of responding to the Father has not fulfilled *their* expectations of the one who would redeem Israel. In fact, they know all that one might be expected to know about Jesus, right down to the Easter message. They know of his life: Jesus of Nazareth, a prophet mighty in word and deed (v. 19).[42] They know of his death: 'Our chief priests and rulers delivered him up to be condemned to death, and crucified him' (v. 20). They know of the events at the tomb: 'it is now the third day' (v. 21), women have been at the tomb early in the morning, but 'they did not find his

---

[39] On the eucharistic texts in Acts, see P. H. Menoud, 'The Acts of the Apostles and the Eucharist', in *Jesus Christ and the Faith: A Collection of Studies by Philippe H. Menoud* (Pittsburgh Theological Monograph Series 18; Pittsburgh: Pickwick Press, 1978) pp. 84–106. Menoud argues that 16:34 is also concerned with 'the table of the Lord' (see pp. 89–90).

[40] For detail, see R. J. Dillon, *From Eye-Witnesses to Ministers of the Word* (Analecta Biblica 82; Rome: Biblical Institute Press, 1978) pp. 89–91.

[41] Remarkably, none of the recent commentators see the importance of Luke's deliberate insertion of *apo Ierousalêm*. See, for example, I. H. Marshall, *The Gospel of Luke: A Commentary on the Greek Text* (The New International Greek Testament Commentary; Exeter: Paternoster Press, 1978) pp. 892–3; E. Schweizer, *The Good News According to Luke* (London: SPCK, 1984) p. 370. There is a hint of it in Schweizer's passing parallel between the disciples' departure (vv. 13–14) and return (vv. 33–35) on p. 368. Fitzmyer, *Luke X–XXIV*, p. 1562 argues that Emmaus is mentioned because it is 'in the vicinity of Jerusalem', and thus there is no journey away from Jerusalem. Similarly, see Dillon, *From Eye-Witnesses*, pp. 85–6.

[42] For an excellent study of the Lucan Christology involved in the disciples' description of Jesus, see Dillon, *From Eye-Witnesses*, pp. 111–45.

body' (v. 23). They have even heard the Easter proclamation: there has been a vision of angels who said: 'He is alive!' (v. 23). These disciples *know* everything, but him they did not see, and thus they have had enough. They continue their walk away from Jerusalem.[43]

Reflecting the practice of the Lucan Church we read of a long liturgy of the word, as Jesus 'interpreted to them in all the scriptures the things concerning himself' (v. 27). It is with these failed disciples who have abandoned God's journey that Jesus journeys and with whom he will eventually join in Eucharist. However, it is important to notice that, after the liturgy of the word, and before the breaking of the bread, initiative must come from the erring disciples themselves. The RSV translation of 24:28 reads: 'He appeared to be going further', but this misses an important point. The Greek verb is more suggestive (*prosepoiêsato*). The story-teller indicates that 'he *pretended* to be going further'. In other words, he has done his part in unfolding God's plan through the explanation of the Scriptures. The disciples must now take some initiative. They respond generously: 'Stay with us for it is toward evening, and the day is now far spent' (v. 29). The littleness of faith that has led them to leave Jerusalem and the eleven is gradually being overcome by the presence of the Risen Lord. The process of repentance and the forgiveness (v. 47) is under way.

At the meal the disciples recognised him in the breaking of the bread (vv. 30–31). Jesus has set out to follow and to journey with these failing disciples, as they walked away from God. He has come to meet them, to make himself known to them and to draw them back to the journey of God through opening the word of God to them, and through the breaking of the bread.[44] 'Jesus shares the new life of the resurrection of the just by breaking bread for two disciples who have abandoned his way of justice.'[45]

Touched in their failure, the immediate reaction of the failed disciples is to turn back on their journey: 'And they rose that same

---

[43] Their knowledge of the 'brute facts' of the resurrection story is widely recognised. For a suggestive analysis of what this means for Lucan thought, see Dillon, *From Eye-Witnesses*, pp. 55–6, 110–11.

[44] For a fully documented discussion of the eucharistic character of 24:30, see J. Dupont, 'The Meal at Emmaus', in J. Delorme *et al.*, *The Eucharist in the New Testament* (London: Geoffrey Chapman, 1965) pp. 115–21. The article runs from 105–121. See also Dillon, *From Eye-Witnesses*, pp. 149–55. Dillon has further pointed out that in both Luke and Acts 'breaking of the bread' is associated with instruction concerning Jesus' person and mission.

[45] Karris, *Luke*, p. 48.

hour and returned to Jerusalem' (v. 33).[46] Once they arrive back to
the place which they should never have abandoned and the eleven
upon whom the community is founded, they find that Easter faith is
already alive. They are told: 'The Lord has risen indeed, and has
appeared to Simon' (v. 34).

The use of the name 'Simon' is important for our argument. As
the Gospel opens, the reader comes to know of a man called 'Simon'
(4:38). Within the context of a miraculous catch of fish he is called to
be a disciple of Jesus, and Jesus introduces a new name for him,
'Peter' (see 5:8). The reader is immediately reminded of this transfor-
mation in Luke's list of the twelve apostles: 'Simon, whom he
named Peter' (6:14). From that point on, throughout the whole of
the Gospel, he is called 'Peter' (see 8:45, 51; 9:20, 28, 32–33; 12:41;
18:28). Even at the Last Supper, where the mingling of the themes of
Jesus' sharing his table with the broken and the commissioning of
his future apostles is found, he is still 'Peter' (22:8, 34, 54, 55, 58, 60–
61).

Yet, in foretelling his denials, Jesus emphatically reverts to the
name he had before he became a disciple: 'Simon, Simon, behold,
Satan demanded to have you that he might sift you like wheat'
(22:31). The return to 'Peter' at the end of Jesus' words is, in itself, a
sign that all is not lost (v. 34). Yet it is to the failed Simon that the
Risen Lord has appeared, to restore him to his apostolic role (24:34).
The name 'Simon', without any contact with the name 'Peter',
appears only before this man's call to be a follower of Jesus (4:18)
and at the end of the Emmaus story, when two failing disciples are
restored to God's saving story, which is taking place in Jerusalem.
There another sinner, Simon, has also been blessed by the presence
of the Risen Lord (23:34).[47]

The failed disciples have come back home to another disciple
who had failed his Lord. This return home, however, has happened
because the Lord has reached out to them in their brokenness, and
made himself known to them in the breaking of the bread:

---

[46] The fact that they 'return to Jerusalem' in v. 33 further enhances the importance of
their travelling 'away from Jerusalem' in v. 13. Many scholars have seen the theological importance of this 'return'. For detail of this scholarship, see Dillon, *From Eye-
Witnesses*, pp. 92–4. Dillon finds himself in difficulty here. He has not appreciated the
importance of the going 'away from Jerusalem' in v. 13, and thus can only be
'tentatively affirmative' (p. 93) to these suggestions.

[47] Unfortunately, most scholars see this return to 'Simon' as an indication of the
traditional nature of 24:34 (see 1 Cor. 15:4). See, for example, Fitzmyer, *Luke X–
XXIV*, p. 1569: 'a stereotyped formula for appearances'. I am suggesting that there is a
more subtle Lucan point at stake. For a similar suggestion, see Dillon, *From Eye-
Witnesses*, p. 100, note 88. See also Tannehill, *Narrative Unity*, pp. 292–3.

> Here ... we find Jesus eating with outcasts, but this time the outcasts are two of his own disciples who have abandoned their journey of faith, fled Jerusalem, and embarked on their own journey. Jesus crosses the boundaries of disloyalty and breaks the bread of reconciliation with these disciples. Strengthened by the risen Jesus, Cleopas and his companion hasten back to Jerusalem and rejoin the journey of discipleship.[48]

In his own unique way, the Evangelist Luke has taken up the traditional message of the Eucharist as the presence of Jesus to the broken and remoulded it to fit his even more complex situation of sinners, disciples with inadequate faith, failing apostles, Gentiles and self-righteous Jews. Two disciples with inadequate faith had decided to walk 'away from Jerusalem' (v. 13), and the Easter proclamation announced the presence of the Risen Lord to the failed Simon: 'The Lord has risen indeed, and has appeared to Simon' (v. 34).

The return of the two disciples from Emmaus to Jerusalem leads into Jesus' final meal, celebrated with the eleven in the upper room (24:36–43).[49] Although 'the scene is intended to stress the identity and the physical reality of the risen Christ who has appeared to his disciples',[50] there are close parallels between the experience of the eleven and the experience of the Emmaus disciples which are instructive.[51]

EMMAUS	JERUSALEM
Talking to each other (v. 14).	Talking to each other (v. 35).
Jesus appears (v. 15).	Jesus appears (v. 36).
He is not recognised (v. 16).	He is not recognised (v. 37).
Jesus asks a rhetorical question (vv. 25–26).	Jesus asks a rhetorical question (v. 38–40).
Instruction based on Scripture (v. 27).	Instruction based on Scripture (vv. 44–49).
Revealing actions with bread (vv. 30–31).	Revealing actions with bread and fish (vv. 41–42).
Jesus disappears (v. 31).	Jesus disappears (v. 51).
The disciples return to Jerusalem (v. 33).	The apostles return to Jerusalem (v. 52).

[48] R. J. Karris, 'God's Boundary-Breaking Mercy', *Bible Today* 24 (1986) 27–8 (whole article: pp. 24–9). See also D. Senior & C. Stuhlmueller, *The Biblical Foundations for Mission* (New York: Orbis Books, 1983) pp. 266–7.

[49] Although he does not discuss the eucharistic nature of this scene, the importance of the table-fellowship has been shown by D. R. Dumm, 'Luke 24:44–49 and Hospitality', in D. Durkin (ed.), *Sin, Salvation and the Spirit: Commemorating the Fiftieth Year of the Liturgical Press* (Collegeville: Liturgical Press, 1979) pp. 230–9.

The close parallels between 24:13–35 and 36–52 suggest that this final meal is not only the reconstitution of a failed discipleship and a commissioning of the apostles. Luke has carefully linked the final meals at Emmaus and Jerusalem, and this might be a hint that both are eucharistic. Through his use of bread and fish he has also been able to link the final commission to the eleven and his initial formation of that same group in 9:10–17, where he had earlier given them bread and fish (9:16).

Jesus drew the disciples who had lost their way at Emmaus back to Jerusalem through a eucharistic table. He now commissions his apostles to witness repentance and the forgiveness of sins to all the nations (vv. 44–49) at a eucharistic table. The fellowship at table that has been broken by the sinfulness and frailty of the apostles has been definitively re-established. They have experienced the reality of their own brokenness. They have now further experienced the loving presence of the Risen Lord at the eucharistic table leading them to the repentance and forgiveness of sins, which they are commissioned to witness to all the nations (v. 47).[52]

Conclusion

Luke has no hesitation in setting the eucharistic presence of the Lord in the midst of many of the followers of Jesus who could be described as 'broken': sinners, unfaithful disciples, failing apostles, physically impure and Gentiles. His account of the feeding of the multitudes with bread (9:10–17), although eucharistic, does not repeat the Marcan and Matthean questions to their communities of disciples who are not sufficiently open to the ways of the Lord. It is used for the formation of future missionaries, the twelve apostles who will feed all the nations. However, his widespread use of table settings to provide the contexts for Jesus' radical questioning of the status quo paves the way for the meals that conclude Luke's story of Jesus.

Both in the Last Supper and at the table at Emmaus they are failed and sinful disciples who are touched by the presence of the Lord. At the Last Supper (22:14–38) Luke has used the overall background of his many meals to indicate that even here he is prepared to call to himself the broken people.

However, into this background he has inserted the tradition of a farewell discourse. The blending of these two features, the meals of

---

[50] Fitzmyer, *Luke X–XXIV*, p. 1575.

[51] I am grateful to Mark Coleridge for this insight.

[52] On this, see Dillon, *From Eye-Witnesses*, pp. 197–203. See also Idem, 'Easter Revelation and Mission Program in Luke 24:46–48', in Durkin, *Sin, Salvation and the Spirit*, pp. 240–70.

instructions for the future are given to a group of squabbling disciples (vv. 24–30), and he commissions Peter, who will deny him (vv. 31–34). This leads to a rather impure form of the 'farewell discourse' tradition. Luke intends it to be precisely that. Through this blending of the two features, he is able to show that, sinners though they may be, the people at the table will eventually become the apostles, and thus living witnesses to repentance and the forgiveness of sins (24:47). What is important for Luke is that these apostles 'witness' to something that they have experienced.

On the eventful 'day' of the resurrection, sinful disciples, discouraged by the strange ways of God, who decreed that the Messiah must suffer many things (see 9:22; 22:22; 24:26, 46), walk away from Jerusalem. Through the liturgy of the journey to Emmaus these disciples are called back to the way of the Lord, symbolically centred upon the city that is, in fact, the central point, where God leads Jesus back to himself and whence the apostles are sent to all the nations. Jesus sets out after his failing disciples, and calls them back to himself through the breaking of the bread (24:13–35). Throughout the Gospel, at the Last Supper, and finally at Emmaus, Jesus shares his table with the broken.[53]

From the material we have studied, I would like to suggest that through his special version of the last meal (22:14–38), and his addition of the Emmaus journey to the traditional resurrection stories of an empty tomb, appearances and a commission,[54] Luke has taken the early Church's understanding of the Eucharist as Jesus' presence to the broken to even greater depths.

---

[53] There is a growing sensitivity among scholars of Luke's special interest in the 'lost ones'. This has always been noticed as central to the three parables in Luke 15, but the theme is now seen as all-pervasive. See especially, Donahue, *The Gospel in Parable*, pp. 126–93. With particular reference to the way in which the Emmaus story embodies a theme that runs through the whole Gospel, see Dillon, *From Eye-Witnesses*, pp. 240–9. Interestingly (for our purposes), Dillon entitles this section of his study: 'Guest and host of the unworthy'. More generally, see R. I. Cassidy, *Jesus, Politics and Society: A Study of Luke's Gospel* (Maryknoll: Orbis Books, 1980); J. Massyngbaerde Ford, *My Enemy is My Guest: Jesus and Violence in Luke* (Maryknoll: Orbis Books, 1984); O'Toole, *Luke's Theology*, pp. 109–48; Karris, *Luke*, pp. 23–78.

[54] For a basic study of the constitutive elements of resurrection stories, see C. H. Dodd, 'The Appearances of the Risen Christ: An Essay in Form-Criticism of the Gospels', in *More New Testament Studies* (Manchester: Manchester University Press, 1968) pp. 102–33. See also, R. E. Brown, *The Virginal Conception and Bodily Resurrection of Jesus* (London: Geoffrey Chapman, 1973) pp. 96–125.

CHAPTER FIVE

The Fourth Gospel

Our study of the eucharistic material in the three Synoptic Gospels (Mark, Matthew and Luke) has shown that these Evangelists tell the basic story of Jesus in their own way. When we turn to the Fourth Gospel, we find ourselves moving in a different world.[1] The overall story hardly ever fits the scheme of the Synoptic Gospels, and John's understanding of the life, preaching, death and resurrection of Jesus is unique.[2]

John is convinced that God gave to the world, which he loves, the gift of his Son. He gave this gift so that the world might have life (see John 3:16). Does this 'gift' manifest itself in the world and in the Church through the presence of Jesus in the Eucharist? Is there a 'eucharistic theology' in the Fourth Gospel? Our attempts to answer these questions will lead us beyond the traditional stories of the

---

[1] I see the Fourth Gospel as the product of a long history. It is the result of great originality in combining traditional 'stories' and other sources with a more unique Johannine contribution. The final document, which would have appeared about 100 CE, is arguably the most subtle theological work in the New Testament. In what follows, I shall use the terms 'John' and 'Johannine' without implying anything about the precise identity of the author(s).

[2] For a recent study showing this, see F. J. Moloney, article 'Johannine Theology', in R. E. Brown, J. A. Fitzmyer & R. E. Murphy (eds), *The New Jerome Biblical Commentary* (Englewood Cliffs: Prentice-Hall, 1989) pp. 1417–26.

Jesus and the farewell discourse, produces its own difficulties. Jesus' multiplication of the bread, and of the words over the bread and the wine at the Last Supper.

Contemporary interpretations of the Fourth Gospel take a wide variety of opposing positions about the presence or absence of sacramental teaching in this Gospel. Some scholars have argued for an understanding of many of the events from the life of Jesus as deeply impregnated with a sacramental understanding of God's action in Jesus. Where there is the possibility of sacramental teaching, then we must take it for granted that John implies such teaching.[3] Others have claimed that John has no interest in the idea of sacraments, and may well be 'anti-sacramental'.[4] We cannot survey this scholarship within the pages of this study.[5]

Some contemporary scholars find 'hints' of eucharistic teaching throughout this beautiful but subtle Gospel. The miracle of the marriage feast at Cana (John 2:1–11) has to be interpreted symbolically to see the wine that Jesus provides as eucharistic. The Johannine version of the miracle of the multiplication of the bread (6:1–13), like the Synoptic stories, reflects a eucharistic background. The people 'recline' for a meal (vv. 10–11), Jesus 'takes', 'gives thanks' (Greek *eucharistêsas*), and only in John does Jesus himself make the distribution of both the bread and the fish (v. 11). However, the 'sign' of the bread is misunderstood. Seeing this event as an eschatological gift of the second Manna from the Mosaic-like prophet, the people cry out: 'This is indeed the prophet who is to come into this world' (v. 14). Thus Jesus withdraws, 'perceiving that they were about to come and take him by force to make him king' (v. 15). As often with the Johannine miracles the misunderstanding of the sign leads into the discourse on the bread from heaven (vv. 25–59).[6] A symbolic reading of the Gospel has also been applied to Jesus' gift

---

[3] Especially important has been the work of O. Cullmann, *Early Christian Worship* (Studies in Biblical Theology 10; London: SCM Press, 1953).

[4] The classical statement of this position is found in H. Odeberg, *The Fourth Gospel: Interpreted in Relation to Contemporaneous Religious Currents in Palestine and the Hellenistic-Oriental World* (Uppsala: Almqvist, 1929). On John 6, see pp. 235–69.

[5] Excellent surveys can be found in the older but still valuable work of W. F. Howard & C. K. Barrett, *The Fourth Gospel in Recent Criticism* (London: Epworth Press, 1955) pp. 195–212, and the more recent study of R. Kysar, *The Fourth Evangelist and His Gospel: An Examination of Contemporary Scholarship* (Minneapolis: Augsburg, 1975) pp. 249–62.

[6] See E. Lohse, 'Miracles in the Fourth Gospel', in M. Hooker & C. Hickling (eds), *What About the New Testament? Essays in Honour of Christopher Evans* (London: SCM Press, 1975) pp. 64–75. See also Léon-Dufour, 'Les miracles de Jésus selon Jean', in AA.VV, *Les Miracles de Jésus selon le Nouveau Testament* (Parole de Dieu; Paris: Editions du Seuil, 1977) pp. 269–86.

of himself at the footwashing as 'analogous in content with the context of the narrative of the supper'.[7] The allegory on the vine (15:1–5) is sometimes seen as eucharistic in its use of the theme of 'abiding'.[8]

Whatever may be the case with the possible 'hints' throughout the Gospel, in agreement with many scholars I believe that a theology of the Eucharist plays an important role in 6:51c–58 and 19:34.[9] The section of the discourse on the bread of life (6:25–59) where Jesus speaks explicitly of eating the flesh of the Son of Man and drinking his blood (i.e. vv. 51c–58) faces real problems, which existed within the Johannine community. Throughout the discourse on the bread from heaven which/who would give life, Jesus has insisted: 'Everyone who sees the Son and believes in him should have eternal life . . . He who believes has eternal life' (vv. 40, 46; see also vv. 35–36). At the end of the first century, the Johannine community can justifiably ask: where is this Son that we may see him? They are told, in the explicitly eucharistic teaching of vv. 51–58, to make that decision in their celebration of the Eucharist, in their eating the flesh and drinking the blood of the Son of Man. It is in the broken body and the spilt blood of the eucharistic celebration that they shall 'look on him whom they have pierced' (19:37).[10]

The same point is made as the Evangelist tells of the blood and water flowing from the pierced side of the crucified Jesus (19:34). It is insufficient simply to develop a theology of the Cross that sees Jesus being lifted up and exalted (see 3:13–15; 8:28; 12:23, 32–33), glorifying the Father (7:37–39; 12:28; 13:31–32; etc.). This raises a further question. Where can the Johannine community (and the

---

[7] S. Schneiders, 'The Footwashing (John 13:1–20): An Experiment in Hermeneutics', *Catholic Biblical Quarterly* 43 (1981) 81, note 22. See pp. 80–1. This fine article runs from pp. 76–92.

[8] Kodell, *Eucharist*, pp. 118–20, 126–9. For a criticism of the over-use of the Fourth Gospel in this sense, see Léon-Dufour, *Sharing*, pp. 272–5. However, this must be read in terms of pp. 261–7, where Léon-Dufour develops his own 'symbolic reading' of John in order fully to understand him. See also Idem, 'Towards a Symbolic Reading of the Fourth Gospel', *New Testament Studies* 27 (1980–81) 439–56.

[9] See F. J. Moloney, 'When is John Talking about Sacraments?', *Australian Biblical Review* 30 (1982) 10–33. Documentation and discussion of the various scholarly positions can be found in this article. Schneiders, 'The Footwashing', p. 81, note 22 creates a useful distinction between material that is 'equivalent in content' and 'analogous in function'. I would claim that 6:51–58 and 19:34 are 'equivalent in content', and in this sense 'eucharistic'.

[10] See F. J. Moloney, 'John 6 and the Celebration of the Eucharist', *Downside Review* 93 (1975) 243–51 and Idem, *The Johannine Son of Man* (Biblioteca di Scienze Religiose 14: Rome, LAS, 1978) pp. 87–107. Brown, *John*, p. 287 rightly claims that 'the backbone of vss. 51–58 is made up of material from the Johannine narrative of the institution of the Eucharist'.

Church of all those 'who have not seen and yet believe' [20:29]) find and experience this revelation of God upon the Cross? The answer is found in the Evangelist's insistence, as he tells of the blood and water flowing from the side of the pierced Jesus, 'that you also may believe' (19:35). Again this Evangelist responds to the needs of his community by telling its members that they will find the presence of the pierced one in their eucharistic celebrations.[11]

My sketch indicates that the two major eucharistic texts of the Fourth Gospel develop a theological and pastoral approach so far not identified in our study. There is an understanding of Eucharist as 'presence', as throughout the other gospels, but this Evangelist adapts that theology to address the needs of a community sensing its distance from the saving events of the life and death of Jesus. Thus these passages continue John's basic teaching on the sacraments: 'It is in the Sacraments of Baptism and Eucharist that the Johannine Church can find the presence of the absent one'.[12]

This message was clearly addressed to a community wondering (at the end of the first century) where and how they might encounter the Christ, the Son of God, so as to come to a deeper faith in him (see 20:31). John was offering a significant response to a troubled community.[13] The theme of 'presence' is evident, but one cannot claim that these classical eucharistic passages from the Fourth Gospel carry the theme found in Mark, Matthew and Luke: the Eucharist as the presence of Jesus to the broken.

Are we to conclude, therefore, that the eucharistic practice, and the traditions that formed part of the life of this particular Church at the end of the first century, either did not know or had abandoned such an understanding of Jesus' eucharistic presence to his pilgrim Church? While there is a clear understanding of the Eucharist as Jesus' presence to the broken in Matthew, Mark and Luke, must we conclude that this is not the case for John? Is his understanding of Eucharist so concerned with a theology of 'the presence of the absent one' that the theme of a total gift of self in love (even to those who fail) does not appear?

Another passage in the Fourth Gospel, sometimes suggested as

---

[11] E. Malatesta, 'Blood and Water from the Pierced Side of Christ', in P.-R. Tragan (ed.), *Segni e Sacramenti nel Vangelo di Giovanni* (Studia Anselmiana 66; Rome: Editrice Anselmiana, 1977) pp. 164–81.

[12] Moloney, 'When is John Talking about Sacraments?', p. 25 (see also pp. 23–5).

[13] Just what these 'troubles' were is at the heart of a great deal of contemporary Johannine research. See, for some exciting suggestions, R. E. Brown, *The Community of the Beloved Disciple: The Life, Loves and Hates of an Individual Church in New Testament Times* (London: Geoffrey Chapman, 1979).

'sacramental', deserves our special attention: the narrative of the footwashing and the gift of the morsel in John 13:1–38.[14] After the solemn announcement that Jesus, knowing his hour had come to return to the Father, is about to show his remarkable love for his own 'unto the end' (13:1),[15] a footwashing and a meal are reported. The footwashing has baptismal hints (see especially 13:6–11).[16]

Traditionally this meal has been understood as eucharistic, in the light of the account of the Last Supper in all three Synoptic Gospels. Mark, Matthew and Luke, as we have seen, all situate Jesus' gift of bread and wine as his body and blood within the context of his Last Supper with his disciples. The situation is more complicated in the Fourth Gospel. Never do we find an account that parallels the setting and the ceremony at the table reported by the Synoptic Gospels. In a quite different setting, in a discourse beside the lake of Tiberias (see 6:1), we find words that vaguely recall that night. Jesus tells his disciples and 'the Jews': 'The bread which I shall give is my flesh for the life of the world' (6:51).[17]

The Problem of the Last Discourse and John 13:1–38

Although there is no report of Jesus' words and actions over broken bread and over a shared cup given to his disciples, John 13–17 is deliberately set at a meal table (see 13:2, 4, 12, 21–30; 14:31). We need to look carefully at the Johannine version of the Last Supper and Discourse, to test whether in his subtle way the Fourth Evangelist has continued a eucharistic tradition through this part of the narrative. The analysis of John 13–17 is fraught with difficulties, which we need to mention at this stage of our study.

One of the more perplexing problems facing the interpreter of the Fourth Gospel is the unevenness, the repetitions and other unusual

---

[14] For a good discussion of the possible sacramental interpretation of John 13, see R. Schnackenburg, *The Gospel According to St John* (Herder's Theological Commentary on the New Testament; London/New York: Burns & Oates/Crossroad, 1968–82) vol. 3, pp. 39–47.

[15] The Greek expression *eis telos* has a double meaning. It means both that he loved his own till the end of his life (chronologically) and also that he loved them in a way that has no bounds (qualitatively).

[16] See, among many, B. Lindars, *The Gospel of John* (New Century Bible; London: Oliphants, 1972) pp. 451–2; C. K. Barrett, *The Gospel According to St John* (London: SPCK, 1978) pp. 441–2. The issue is well surveyed in R. E. Brown, *The Gospel According to John* (Anchor Bible 29–29A; New York: Doubleday, 1966–70) pp. 558–9.

[17] It is widely accepted that this formula embodies part of the eucharistic words that would have been used at the celebrations of the Johannine Community. On this, see Brown, *John*, pp. 284–5; Jeremias, *Eucharistic Words*, pp. 117–18.

features of John's so-called Last Discourse (John 13:1–17:26).[18] The most immediately recognised of these is the apparent decision to finish the discourse and to leave the setting of the meal celebrated in the upper room in 14:31: 'Rise, let us go hence'. This passage would link very well with the first verse of the passion narrative in 18:1: 'When Jesus had spoken these words, he went forth with his disciples across the Kidron valley.' Inexplicably, despite Jesus' words previous to the command to 'go hence', 'I will no longer talk much with you' (14:30), he launches into the allegory on the true vine (15:1–11) — and much else — without any indication of a time, place or situation for the material that runs from 15:1–16:33.

A similar potential conclusion to the whole discourse can be found in 16:32–33:

> The hour is coming, indeed it has come, when you will be scattered, every man to his home, and will leave me alone; yet I am not alone, for the Father is with me. I have said this to you, that in me you may have peace. In the world you have tribulation; but be of good cheer, I have overcome the world.

These words could also serve as a stirring and profoundly Johannine introduction to the passion narrative, but they inexplicably lead into the prayer of Jesus' hour (17:1–26).[19]

These are some of the more outstanding difficulties, but they are some indication why, most recently, a scholar who has devoted great energy to the study of John 13–17, Fernando Segovia, could write: 'Nowadays hardly any exegete would vigorously maintain that John 13:31–18:1 constitutes a literary unity as it stands.'[20] The words of Segovia indicate another widely held position as regards the Last Discourse: that it begins with 13:31. Most scholars would see 13:1–30 as a narrative, telling of the footwashing and of the gift of the morsel, while vv. 31–32 provide the solemn opening of the discourse proper.

Certainly there are difficulties in reading the whole of the discourse as a unit, but, as I have suggested, many similar difficulties are found within John 13:1–38 itself. There appears to be a double interpretation of the footwashing scene. The first of these, from v. 4 to v. 11, speaks of the disciple's 'having a part' in the death of Jesus,

---

[18] For a good survey, see Brown, *John*, pp. 581–604.

[19] For this title, and a short explanation of John 17, see F. J. Moloney, 'John 17: The Prayer of Jesus' Hour', *Clergy Review* 67 (1982) 79–83.

[20] Fernando F. Segovia, *Love Relationships in the Johannine Tradition: Agapê/Agapan in I John and the Fourth Gospel* (SBL Dissertation Series 58; Chico: Scholars Press, 1982) p. 82. On John 13, see Idem, 'John 13:1–20, The Footwashing in the Johannine Tradition', *Zeitschrift für die Neutestamentliche Wissenschaft* 73 (1982) 31–51.

with possible baptismal contacts. This theme disappears in v. 12. From v. 12 to v. 20 the idea seems to be more concerned with 'morality'. It is a more exhortative passage written to encourage the imitation of Jesus. Because it is judged as 'moralistic' in tone, it is often seen to be a later addition. The original version was a more theological reflection on Jesus' gift of himself to his disciples in love, and his invitation of the disciples to join him in that loving gift of self. The baptismal hints are embedded in this view of 'having part' with Jesus' gift of himself.

As mentioned already, it is also widely accepted that vv. 31–38 should be separated from the more narrative accounts of the foot-washing and the gift of the morsel. It seems clumsy of the Evangelist to mention Judas' ominous departure from the upper room, into the darkness (v. 30) with Jesus' exultant proclamation:

> Now is the Son of Man glorified and in him God is glorified; if God is glorified in him, God will glorify him in himself, and glorify him at once. (vv. 31–32)

This proclamation of the glorification of the Son of Man is judged to be the beginning of the discourse proper. Some scholars understand vv. 31–38 as the original introduction to 13:31–14:31, the more primitive form of the discourse,[21] while others see it as a solemn introductory summary of the whole of the discourse in its final form.[22]

Our closer look at the details of the Last Discourse in general, and 13:31–38 in particular, is confusing. We seem to be dealing with a muddle of suggestions and hypotheses about the original discourse, later additions to that discourse, and many other theories. Indeed, the tensions that appear in John 13:1–17:26 have led to a growing tendency to rediscover various strata, reflecting different stages in the Johannine community's experience and reflection. At various stages over the seventy years of life that this Christian community had before the gospel finally appeared in its present form, Jesus' discourses would have been told time and time again. The Last Discourse (of 13:1–17:26) is a final collection of many of those discourses that had been originally remembered and told in various times and situations throughout the life of the Johannine Church.[23]

This has been a helpful and healthy approach to a difficult problem. Rather than assigning different sections of the discourse to

---

[21] See, for example, Brown, *John*, pp. 605–16.

[22] See, for example, Barrett, *St John*, pp. 449–53.

[23] This approach has been expertly and sensitively used in the major commentaries of Schnackenburg and Brown.

'later insertions' or any such derogatory term, an attempt is made to link the strata that can be found throughout the passage with various stages in the history of the community's faith development. As the members of the community needed to find solutions to the difficulties aroused by the opposition, the sinfulness and the new situations that they encountered in their own faith journey, they turned to their memories of Jesus' discourses, and told them again and again. Thus the Last Discourse can be used as a source for the rediscovery of the history of the Johannine community.[24]

I have no doubt that the Last Discourse of the Fourth Gospel had a long and complicated literary history, and that we can trace that history, reflecting the history of the community itself, through careful analysis. Yet I have been led further to believe that whoever may have been responsible for the shape of the Last Discourse as we now have it was a person of great skill. The Fourth Evangelist consciously took these various strata from the recorded memory of his community and laid them side by side to form the Last Discourse. This process may have been repeated many times until the Gospel as we now have it was eventually produced. Because of this process, the final product, even though it sometimes has untidy seams, is thoroughly Johannine in all its parts.[25]

The practice of telling stories, handing them down from generation to generation, is not unique to the New Testament. However, the repeated telling of other people's stories eventually leads to their becoming the story-tellers' own.[26] Thus, despite the many contemporary claims to the contrary, it is important to understand 13:1–17:26 as a whole. The same must also be done for the composite parts (in our case 13:1–38) of the discourse. With care and patience, it can be shown to be a most satisfying work from both a literary and theological point of view.[27]

---

[24] A good example of this approach is J. Painter, 'The Farewell Discourses and the History of Johannine Christianity', *New Testament Studies* 27 (1980–81) 525–43. This method has also been extensively used by Segovia, *Love Relationships*. For an earlier survey, see Schnackenburg, *John*, vol. 3, pp. 6–15.

[25] One of the difficulties in separating the strata of the Fourth Gospel lies in the fact that the Gospel *as a whole* has a very unified style and language. This is the result of continual re-working over the decades of the Johannine community's telling and re-telling of the story of Jesus. See Barrett, *St John*, pp. 5–15.

[26] R. T. Fortna, *The Fourth Gospel and Its Predecessor: From Narrative Source to Present Gospel* (Studies of the New Testament and its World; Edinburgh: T. & T. Clark, 1989) writes of John 13: 'The material has been so greatly rewritten, perhaps more than once . . . that reconstruction of the source now seems too tenuous to be practicable.'

[27] I am taking issue here with some scholars who are still very critical of the present state of the Gospel. Commenting on John 13:21–30, E. Haenchen, *John* (Hermeneia; Philadelphia: Fortress Press, 1984) vol. 2, p. 112 writes: 'One of the most remarkable scenes of the Fourth Gospel has been spoiled by a foolish redactor.' I, for one, beg to differ.

The Narrative Design of John 13:1–38

I wish to test my insistence that 13:1–38 is a satisfying work from both a literary and theological point of view. Before any coherent message can be drawn from the passage, we should attempt to discover the literary techniques used by the Fourth Evangelist in the composition of his account of the footwashing and the gift of the morsel in 13:1–38, whatever his sources may have been.

To return to the terminology used in our analysis of the Marcan story of Jesus, we will now consider elements of narrative earlier described as plot, rhetoric and characters. We need to trace the structure of the succession of events and actions described (plot), but we need to do more than that. It is not enough to trace the events of the story. We must also ask why the Evangelist told this particular story *in this way* (rhetoric). Crucial to both the plot and the rhetoric are the people who are involved in the action (characters).

C. H. Dodd once wrote that we must respect the text as it is, and not try to improve upon it, as the text 'was devised by somebody — even if he were only a scribe doing his best'.[28] It appears to me that there is sufficient evidence to show that this scribe's best was very good indeed![29]

1 The Structure of the Overall Plot

The first important matter to be decided is where the passage begins and ends. We have already seen that there is a widespread acceptance that vv. 31–38 belong to the discourse of chapters 14–17, and thus should be separated from the narratives of the footwashing and the morsel. There is no doubt that with 13:1 a decisively new direction is being taken in the narrative. Jesus is now alone with his disciples in the upper room, about to show the immensity of his love.

But where does this passage come to an end? Are we considering only 13:1–30, or did the Evangelist originally intend that vv. 31–38 be read as belonging to the footwashing and the gift of the morsel? The material found in vv. 31–38 is not only discourse. Indeed, there is an important encounter between Simon Peter and Jesus in vv. 36–38, where the future denials of Simon Peter are openly foretold. This passage closely matches the similar prophecy of the future betrayal

---

[28] C. H. Dodd, *The Interpretation of the Fourth Gospel* (Cambridge (UK): Cambridge University Press, 1953) p. 309. See also the good methodological principles outlined by T. Okure, *The Johannine Approach to Mission: A Contextual Study of John 4:1–42* (WUNT 2. Reihe 31; Tübingen: J. C. B. Mohr [Paul Siebeck], 1988) pp. 39–57, 297–306.

[29] I lay no claim to great originality in the structural suggestions that follow. For my analysis of John's 'rhetoric' I am largely following the work of Y. Simoens, *La Gloire d'aimer: structures stylistiques et interprétatives dans la discours de la cène* (Analecta Biblica 90; Rome: Biblical Institute Press, 1981) pp. 81–104.

of Judas in vv. 10–11. A careful analysis of the plot, the rhetoric and the characters of the narrative may well show that there is a close relationship between the prophecies of the betrayal of Judas and the denials of Peter. Let us begin our analysis on the basis of this working hypothesis.

One of the features of the passage is the regular appearance of a typically Johannine expression: 'Amen, amen I say to you' (see vv. 16, 20, 21, 38). This expression is found *only* in the Fourth Gospel, where it appears twenty-four times.[30] It appears in 13:1–38 more times (four uses) than in any other chapter of the whole Gospel, and it appears only three more times in the Last Discourse (14:12; 16:20, 23).

The fact that the second reference to the betrayal by Judas (v. 21) opens with this expression, while the prophecy of the denials of Peter closes with it (v. 38) shows the author at work. It is the first important indication that John wants to hold together these two examples of the disciples' failure. The use of the very Johannine expression 'amen, amen I say to you', at the beginning and the end of the prophecies of betrayal and denial reported in vv. 21–38 keeps vv. 31–38 closely associated with 13:1–30, rather than the rest of the discourse in chapters 14–17. The theme of the failure of both Judas and Peter does not reappear until the passion narrative (18:1–11, 15–18, 25–27).

In fact, the Evangelist's use of the double 'amen', an expression so typically his, serves as a first indication of the particular 'rhetoric' (the basic structure of the material) of this part of his narrative. John has deliberately positioned his double 'amen' sayings to create the following carefully structured plot:

1. vv. 1–17. This section is formed by the narrative of the footwashing and the discussions that surround that narrative. The features of the section are the Evangelist's comments (see v. 2), the dialogue between Jesus and Peter (vv. 6–9) and Jesus' words on Judas (vv. 10–11) the failure and ignorance of the disciples. The section concludes with the double 'amen' in vv. 16–17.

2. vv. 18–20. Here we have only the words of Jesus himself, directed to the disciples. The section forms the literary 'centre' of the Evangelist's structure and concludes with the double 'amen' in v. 20.

3. vv. 21–38. Returning to the same form as vv. 1–17 we again have narrative and dialogue. The narrative carries forward the theme of Jesus' gift of the morsel. The themes of betrayal and denial intensify (vv. 21–30, 36–38). This section both opens and closes with a double 'amen' in vv. 21 and 38.

---

[30] It is the double use of the 'amen' that is unique to John. 'Amen, I say to you' is found in the Synoptic Gospels, especially in Matthew (31 times).

There seems to be a deliberate arrangement of the chapter into these three sections. It is not only the use of the double 'amen' that guides us, but also the flow of the argument itself. Limiting myself to the double 'amen', however, there is a minor difficulty in that the first double 'amen' does not come right at the end of vv. 1–17. It opens two statements from Jesus, one about the relationship between servant and master (v. 16) and another about knowing and doing (v. 17).

To understand fully John's technique in this section, one has to look back to the opening verses of the passage. There one finds that the whole of vv. 1–4 comes from the Evangelist himself. He is setting both the scene and the theme. In doing so, he plays on the three themes of (a) Jesus and 'his own', (b) his 'knowing' and (c) his 'doing':

> When Jesus *knew* that his hour had come . . . having loved *his own* who were in the world, he loved them to the end . . . Jesus *knowing* that the Father had given all things into his hands . . . *rose* from the supper, *laid aside* his garments, and *girded himself* with a towel.

Jesus 'knowing' that his hour had come, and that the Father had given all things into his hands, led to an active 'doing': he loves his disciples and he washes their feet. Thus the very first statement of the chapter shows the reader that the 'knowing' and 'doing' of Jesus touch the life of the disciples. The narrative continues with Jesus' washing the feet of his disciples and his calling them to have part with him. At the close of the section, after the solemn introduction of the double 'amen', the disciples are told that they are called to repeat exactly what 'the master' has done:

> If you *know* THESE THINGS
> blessed are you
> if you *do* THESE THINGS.[31]

Thus, the first section of Jesus' encounter with his disciples in the upper room (vv. 1–17) is both an indication of the total gift of Jesus for 'his own', through the footwashing, and a call upon them to be so caught up in the new 'knowledge' given to them through this gesture of love that they will 'do' the same in their own lives.

Of crucial importance to the story-teller here is Jesus' self-gift in love and service for his disciples, which will soon take place on the Cross. The sacrament of Baptism is also evident, sweeping the disciples up into the same self-giving life and death as their Master.

---

[31] The Greek original is well balanced:

> ei TAUTA *oidate*
> makarioi este
> ean *poiête* AUTA

The close association between Jesus' instruction to Peter about having part with him and the privileges of those who have bathed, and thus have no further need of washing, in vv. 9–10 show that the Johannine community's practice and understanding of Baptism is close at hand.[32] There is an intimate link between the Sacrament of Baptism and the Lord's death, into which converts were baptised (see Rom. 6:3).[33]

This close scrutiny of the text makes it obvious that the author was indeed very skilful in his use of literary techniques. Similar careful writing will also be found in the central section of the passage (vv. 18–20). The verb 'to know' appears again in v. 18: 'I know whom I have chosen.' However, another theme is mentioned here that was not found anywhere in vv. 1–17. It is not only Jesus' knowledge that is stressed, but also the fact that he has 'chosen' his disciples. This theme is taken further in v. 20: 'He who receives any one whom I send receives me.' Here the 'chosen ones' are further described as 'any one whom I send'. The closely linked themes of being chosen and being sent mark the beginning and the end of vv. 18–20. These two themes of choosing and sending, surrounding Jesus' statement of how and when the disciples will come to understand who he is ('Then you will know that I am he') in v. 19 form a unit, rounded off by the double 'amen'.

The double 'amen' both opens and closes vv. 21–38. The section is also framed with Jesus' prophecies concerning the failure of members of his innermost circle of friends: the disciples with whom he is sharing his table, Judas (vv. 21–30) and Peter (vv. 36–38). Intertwined through the passage dealing with the betrayal of Judas is the theme of the gift of the morsel. On receiving the morsel, Judas leaves the upper room, and the passion is set in motion.

This is the significance of the introduction to Jesus' exultation in v. 31a: 'When he had gone out . . .' The action of Judas is crucial to John's understanding of the glorification of Jesus through the Cross. If the Cross of Jesus is also his exaltation and the place where he glorifies God, then the exit of Judas to betray Jesus unto death leads logically to vv. 31–32. There is no need to force a major break in the narrative between Judas' exit into the night in v. 30 and the words of Jesus in vv. 31–32. The reference to Judas in v. 31a is there because the Evangelist wants the reader to *link* the two.

Jesus' triumphant proclamation of his own glorification and the glorification of God do not form the opening theme of the discourse

---

[32] Anyone following the text here will notice that many translations add 'except for his feet' to v. 10. This was added by later copyists to solve the problem of further forgiveness of sin after Baptism. For detail, see Moloney, *Johannine Son*, pp. 192–3.

[33] On this, see the eloquent discussion of Dodd, *Interpretation*, pp. 401–2.

that follows. It belongs essentially to what has gone before. Precisely because Jesus shows forth the glory of God in his gift of himself on the Cross, the gift of the new commandment now follows logically. He can now command that his disciples love one another *as he has loved them* (vv. 34–35). The Cross is still the paradigm.

The account of the footwashing and the gift of the morsel found in John 13:1–38 is therefore marked by:

(a) The deliberate use of the Johannine literary characteristic of the double 'amen'.

(b) The opening and the closing of each section with a statement and re-statement of the same themes. In the closing re-statement, the original statement is carried a step farther. The section enclosed within vv. 1–17 is marked by the themes of knowing and doing, vv. 18–20 by choosing and sending, vv. 21–38 by the betrayal and denial of disciples.

(c) A narrative unity that can be traced though the development of the argument pursued within each section of the overall account. The themes of love, gift of self, betrayal, ignorance and denial all point towards Jesus' statement that when all these things take place, then the disciples will know: 'I am he' (v. 19).

The overall narrative plot of John 13:1–38 seems to have been deliberately composed around the three sections that I have outlined: vv. 1–17, 18–20 and 21–38.

2 *The Internal Argument of each Section of the Plot*

Now that we have seen the overall structure of the narrative, we need to look more closely at its component parts. John 13:1–38 is marked by another feature. Unlike any other part of the last discourse there is a deliberate use of the interplay between the 'characters'. There are dialogues between Jesus and others, paired with sections without such dialogue. Merely by following these indications of dialogue and monologue it is possible to trace further the unfolding of the narrative structure.

In the first section (vv. 1–17) there are three clearly distinct elements:

(a) vv. 1–5. An *introduction* to the passion and the footwashing. There are no indications of 'dialogue' in this section. It is made up entirely of the Evangelist's setting of the scene and his descriptions of Jesus' knowledge that flowed into action.

(b) vv. 6–11. A *dialogue* between Jesus and Peter. This section is highlighted by 'Peter said . . . Jesus answered him . . . Peter said . . . Jesus answered him . . .' etc.

(c) vv. 12–17. An *explanation* by Jesus, which opens with 'He said to them . . .', but from then on is totally without dialogue. Jesus' teaching is now directed to all the disciples at the table. He is no longer speaking to one person; all the verbs and pronouns are in the plural.

Leaving aside the central section (vv. 18–20) we now turn to vv. 21–38, which form the closing section of the chapter. Following the same criteria, we can find the same tripartite structure.

(a) vv. 21–26a. An *introduction* to the gift of the morsel to Judas. This section is clearly a literary unit, marked by the discussion that arises between Jesus and the disciples because he has spoken of his oncoming betrayal. The main characters in the dialogue are Jesus, Peter and the Beloved Disciple. It concludes with Jesus' indication: 'It is he to whom I shall give this morsel when I have dipped it' (v. 26a).

(b) vv. 26b–30. The morsel is given to Judas, and Jesus speaks to Judas. The section is marked by *the words of Jesus* to Judas. From v. 26b onwards the only two people at the centre of the action and in the dialogue are Jesus and Judas. The only reference to the rest of the disciples is to tell of their ignorance: 'No one at the table knew why he said this to him' (v. 28).

(c) vv. 31–38 is formed by two parts. First there is the *interpretation* of Jesus, again introduced by the words: 'Jesus said'. This interpretation runs as far as v. 35. In vv. 31–35, opening with 'And when he had gone out . . .', Jesus explains Judas' departure in terms of his own glory. As this glory is his total gift of himself, loving 'to the end' (v. 1), the association with the betrayal that will lead to the Cross is important. It is this form of loving that Jesus passes on in the command to his disciples to love as he has loved them (vv. 34–35). Next (vv. 36–38) a brief dialogue between Simon Peter and Jesus follows, foretelling the denials. Vv. 21–38, opening and closing with the Johannine use of the double 'amen', are also framed by the themes of betrayal (vv. 21–30: Judas) and denial (vv. 36–38: Peter).

Before proceeding to look more closely at vv. 18–20 we need to notice that there are some very interesting contacts between what the Evangelist has carefully constructed in the two flanking sections of vv. 1–17 and 21–38. These contacts can best be brought out through the following scheme:

I. *The footwashing seen in the light of the betrayal.*	II. *The gift of the morsel given in the context of betrayal and denial.*
1. The love of Jesus for his own to its perfection (v. 1). The betrayal (v. 2).	1. Jesus troubled in spirit and his witness (v. 21a). The betrayal (vv. 21b–25).
2. Peter–Jesus (vv. 6–10b). The betrayal (vv. 10c–11).	2. Judas–Jesus (vv. 26b–27). The betrayal (vv. 28–30).
3. The gift of example (vv. 12–17).	3. The gift of love (vv. 31–38).

Although the opening section of the scene in the upper room is devoted to the footwashing (which has clear hints of Baptism) and the closing section to the gift of the morsel (which, I will suggest, can be linked with the Eucharist), my analysis so far indicates that the Evangelist has told each of these stories in much the same way. The full significance of this will emerge as we complete our study of John's skilful writing.

The two flanking narratives (vv. 1–17 and 21–38) stress the love, knowledge and action of Jesus as he gives himself in love to his disciples in the midst of their failure: betrayal and denial. The centrepiece of the whole passage (vv. 18–20) is marked by the themes of Jesus' knowledge of his own, the traitor, and the choosing and sending of the disciples. The same themes continue, but in a somewhat different key.

Structurally and thematically the passage unfolds around v. 19, which is, in fact, the very centre of a chapter with 38 verses.[34] This is best seen through a presentation of the text itself:

v. 18. I am not speaking to you all.
I know whom I have chosen.

It is that the scripture may be fulfilled:
'He who *ate my bread* has lifted his heel against me.'

v.20. Amen, amen I say to you, he who receives anyone whom I sent receives me,

and he who *receives me* receives him who sent me.

v. 19. I tell you this now
before it takes place
that you may believe
when it does take place
that I AM HE.

The whole of John 13:1–38 is constructed around two very similar passages, which deal with the footwashing (vv. 1–17) and the gift of the morsel (vv. 21–38). Forming the central statement between these two flanking narratives (vv. 18–20), John reports Jesus' choosing and sending his disciples. Although brief, the central statement is a recognition of Jesus' choosing and sending disciples who share the table with him, yet raise their heel against him (v. 18b). Read within the whole chapter, Jesus proclaims to his disciples who will betray him that he is telling them these things before they happen. When the denials, betrayals and the death of Jesus have been

---

[34] It is important, however, to remember that our present system of chapters and verses was introduced by Robert Stephanus in 1551. It is not as if John thought of a printed page of 38 verses, making v. 19 his central statement!

perpetrated by the very ones whom he has chosen and sent, then they will come to belief in Jesus as 'I am he'.

3 *The Rhetoric of John 13:1–38*

My analysis of the various narrative techniques used by the Fourth Evangelist can now be summarised through the following schematic presentation of the structure of the whole of John 13:1–38:

vv. 1–17	vv. 21–38
The perfection of love (1).	Jesus troubled — witness (21a).
The betrayal (2).	The betrayal (21b).
The knowledge of Jesus (3).	The ignorance of the disciples (22–25).
The footwashing (4–5).	The gift of the morsel (26a).
Simon and Jesus (6–10).	Jesus and Judas (26b–27).
The betrayal (11).	The betrayal (28–30).
Conclusion to the footwashing (12abc).	Exit of Judas — glorification (31–32).
The gift of example (12d–16).	The gift of mutual love (33–35).
The blessedness of putting into practice such knowledge (17).	The non-putting into practice such knowledge in the denials of Peter (36–38).

vv. 18–20
Jesus' knowledge of his chosen
ones and his sending them
(betrayers and deniers as they are)
as the fulfilment of Scripture
and the revelation of Jesus as:
I AM HE

The Evangelist has used the various elements which help to form a narrative (plot, characters and rhetoric) to tell a story of the footwashing and the gift of the morsel as an introduction to both the Last Discourse and the Passion of Jesus.

The account of the footwashing (vv. 1–17) is marked by the themes of Jesus' knowledge of his own, knowledge even of the betrayer, and his love for them. He washes their feet, and leaves them the gift of his example: 'that you also should do as I have done for you' (v. 15). The account of the gift of the morsel (vv. 21–38) repeats the structure and the themes of the footwashing. He knows his disciples. Not only does he know of his betrayer. He also knows of the future denials of Peter. In the midst of these themes of betrayal and denial Jesus gives two further gifts: the gift of the eucharistic morsel and the gift of the new commandment of love: 'that you love one another; even as I have loved you, that you also love one another' (v. 34).

Between these two parallel passages, the words of Jesus are reported (vv. 18–20). He tells his failing disciples that his loving them in the
midst of their betrayal and denial will reveal him as 'I am he'.

It is on the basis of this literary structure, carefully written to state
and re-state a description of Jesus' knowledge and love of his own
(vv. 1–17 and 21–38), around words of Jesus that explain the purpose
of such loving, that we can trace a further aspect of the early Church's
understanding of the Eucharist.[35]

God's Love is Made Known

We are now able to understand the 'body' of the message of John
13:1–38 because we have taken great care to discover its contours.
They are determined by the literary 'skeleton', which I have attempted to reconstruct. Crucial to this structure is the very centre of
the passage. The whole of the chapter devotes so much attention to
the betrayal and denial of Jesus by the very disciples with whom he
shares his table. Similar attention is given to Jesus' commitment to
these very same disciples, 'his own', loving them until death (13:1),
washing their feet (vv. 4–11) and sharing bread, even with his
betrayer (vv. 21–30).

At the heart of the narrative (vv. 18–20) lies the careful presentation of a remarkable truth. Jesus knows whom he has chosen. These
very ones, whose feet he has washed (vv. 1–17) and who have
received the morsel (vv. 21–38), will turn against him (see v. 18).
These are the ones he has chosen. However, the cruel reality of their
turning against him (vv. 2–3, 10–11, 21–30, 36–38), their lifting
their heel against their host at table (v. 18b), alters nothing. In fact,
he will send them forth as both his representatives and ultimately as
the representatives of his Father (vv. 18a, 20). It is in the acceptance
of these failed, yet loved, disciples that one will receive both Jesus
and the Father (v. 20).[36]

In the mystery of God's love, it is precisely in the abject failure of
both Judas and Peter, those chosen and sent by Jesus, that Jesus'
uniqueness and oneness with God can be seen. His love for his

---

[35] I am claiming to uncover a 'further aspect'. John generally presents the Sacraments
as the presence of the absent one. See above, pp. 00–00. Recently, in a stimulating
study, D. Rensberger, *Johannine Faith and Liberating Community* (Philadelphia: Westminster Press, 1988) pp. 64–86 has shown the impact of the Johannine understanding
of Baptism and Eucharist upon the community's understanding of itself.

[36] For an interesting study of 13:1–30, the disciples' failure and ignorance 'victimises'
the implied reader, who is stung into recognising that her/his own knowledge is not
superior to that of the disciples, see J. L. Staley, *The Print's First Kiss: A Rhetorical
Investigation of the Implied Reader in the Fourth Gospel* (SBL Dissertation Series 82;
Atlanta: Scholars Press, 1988) pp. 107–11.

failing disciples is, above all, the final proof for his claim to be the one who makes God known (see 17:2–3). He does not reveal the love of God through any acclaim gained by a human success story. He reveals the love of God by loving unto death those intimate friends and associates who have betrayed and denied him. This is the message that the Johannine Jesus leaves his disciples, as they gather at his table on the night before he died. It is in these very events, when these things 'take place', that the disciples may come to know and believe that Jesus can claim 'I AM HE'. They will have indeed been loved 'to the end' (13:1) by one whom they have betrayed and denied. Little wonder that the final triumphant words of the Johannine Jesus on the Cross are: 'My task has been brought to its perfection' (19:30, Greek *tetelestai*). He has accomplished the task that the Father gave him to do (see 4:34 and 17:4).

This is a remarkable understanding of God, of Jesus, and of his self-giving love for his disciples. Jesus loves his own so much that he chooses them (v. 18a), and sends them out as his very own presence (v. 20). Yet these loved ones are responsible for his death on a cross (v. 18b). It is precisely in his unconditional gift of himself to people who do not love him that Jesus reveals who he is and what he is doing. He reveals a God who loves (3:16) and who is love (1 John 4:8, 16), but the quality of that love is incomprehensible when measured by human criteria and the limited human experience of love. Revealed here is God's love, which transcends and challenges all human criteria and human experience.[37]

On the Cross, love is revealed. Gazing upon the very one whom they have pierced (see 19:37), they will come to understand just how much God loves them. The prophecy of John 13:19 is not the first time Jesus has indicated that he will reveal the greatness of God's love on the Cross. There is a close relationship between this affirmation and Jesus' announcement earlier in this Gospel: 'When you have lifted up the Son of Man, then you will know that I am he' (8:28).

The Fourth Evangelist regularly uses the expression 'I am he' (Greek *egô eimi*) in direct reference to Jesus (see 8:24, 28, 58; 13:19). The expression has a long history in the literature of Israel. Having its distant roots in the revelation of God's name to Moses in Exodus 3:14, but becoming particularly important in the Prophets (see especially Isaiah 43:10; 45:18), it has always been used to refer to the

---

[37] Schneiders, 'The Footwashing', pp. 84–6 presents three models of service and claims that Jesus' service in the footwashing is evidence of the quality of service between friends. There is a further quality of love that is being shown here: a love unto death of friends who have betrayed you and denied you!

living presence of a God who makes himself known among his people.[38]

By using this formula to refer to himself, Jesus informs his disciples — and John, his community and his subsequent readers (see 20:29) — that only when we see and understand a love that reveals itself in such an extraordinary fashion, loving 'to the end' (13:1) those who betray and deny him in return, can we begin to understand the God made known to us in and through Jesus. When these things happen, when his disciples have betrayed, denied and abandoned him, and he is 'lifted up' on the Cross (see 3:13; 8:28; 12:32), then his disciples of all times will know that Jesus is the revelation of God himself:

> I tell you this now,
> before it takes place,
> that when it does take place
> you may believe that
> I AM HE (13:19).[39]

Was the Morsel Eucharistic?

The message of John 13:1–38 is a powerful message indeed, but is there any need for us to link the gift of the morsel to the celebration of the Eucharist? There do not appear to be any explicitly eucharistic overtones in the story. However, it is the Last Supper, which Jesus shares with his failing disciples, and this supper is traditionally linked with the celebration of the Eucharist.

Understandably, this discussion has bothered interpreters at least since the time of Augustine.[40] In the light of the long-standing

---

[38] See, among many works written on the use of 'I am he' in the Fourth Gospel, P. B. Harner, *The 'I am' of the Fourth Gospel* (Facet Books, Biblical Series 26; Philadelphia: Fortress Press, 1970), and the good summary of Brown, *John*, pp. 533–8.

[39] I have no intention of questioning the value of the scholarship that attempts to rediscover the various strata that stand behind the Last Discourse. However, many scholars simply ignore the importance of the structure and message of the text *as we now have it*. It is interesting to find that Haenchen, *John*, vol. 2, pp. 109–10 regards vv. 18–20 (central in my structure) as 'a later addition . . . a redactional insertion' (p. 109), and that v. 20 'does not belong to this context at all' (p. 110). Even if that is so: why was it inserted, and what does it mean in the text as we now have it? For his final overview of the significance of 13: 1–30, see pp. 110–14, where the love theme is rightly stressed, but the role of the chosen but failing disciples is completely missed.

[40] *Homilies on the Gospel of John*, Tractate LXII. See P. Schaff (ed.), *A Select Library of the Nicene and Post-Nicene Fathers* (Grand Rapids: Eerdmans, 1978. Reprint of the 1888 edition) vol. 7, pp. 312–14. Augustine asks the question, but escapes from the problem by reading the Fourth Gospel with the chronology of Luke 23: 19–21.

tradition that this meal was a celebration of the Eucharist (as is explicit in the Synoptic accounts of the Last Supper), how was it possible that Jesus would give a eucharistic morsel to Judas? Augustine asks how it is possible that immediately after the reception of the Eucharist (v. 26), Satan enters into Judas (v. 27). It is precisely this strange juxtaposition of Jesus' generous gift of himself and the presence of the arch-betrayer that has led interpreters to question the eucharistic nature of the meal.[41] The tradition that saw John 13 as eucharistic in the light of the Synoptic Gospels needed to be questioned.[42]

We should not look to the Synoptic tradition for the solution to this question. Indeed, we must look wider into the specifically *Johannine* argument pursued throughout this chapter.[43] We have seen that 13:1–38 is a carefully presented story, which leads to the message that Jesus is glorified (vv. 31–32), that he shines forth as the revelation of God (*egō eimi*), in his unconditional love for those who do not love him, but who, on the contrary, betray and deny him (vv. 18–20). No narrative could portray such love better than a story telling that Jesus of Nazareth, on the night before he died, gave the eucharistic morsel to the very one who would betray him.

However powerful such an argument may be, it is not sufficient to establish the eucharistic nature of the narrative of the gift of the morsel. The method we have used has been to attempt to understand the overall thrust of the argument pursued by the narrative of John 13:1–38 seen as a whole. From those general impressions I have moved to the 'particular' of the morsel in terms of the 'overall' message of God's being revealed in the unconditional love of his Son. While helpful, such arguments lack weight. One needs more evidence *in the detail of the text itself* indicating that the Evangelist wanted the readers to understand this part of his narrative as a reference to the Eucharist. Subtle though the Fourth Evangelist may be, he would have made his point more clearly if he intended his readers to see vv. 21–30 as eucharistic.

---

[41] For an excellent presentation of the discussion, see M.-J. Lagrange, *Evangile selon Saint Jean* (Etudes Bibliques; Paris: Gabalda, 1927) pp. 362–3. Most modern scholars either regard the use of the morsel as a method of eliminating Judas from the upper room (e.g. Schnackenburg, *St John*, vol. 3, p. 30) or as an indication that here Judas chooses Satan rather than Jesus (e.g. Brown, *John*, p. 578).

[42] For a discussion along these lines, see Brown, *John*, pp. 575 and 578.

[43] It is because the full implications of the Johannine argument of the revelation of Jesus' love for his failing disciples *eis telos* have not been given full weight that scholars shy clear of the eucharistic interpretation of the passage. Those who have seen it as eucharistic (e.g. A. Loisy and W. Bauer) use 1 Cor. 11:29 to claim that Satan enters Judas because he takes the eucharistic morsel without discerning. They miss the point entirely. For the discussion, see Brown, *John*, p. 575 and Lagrange, *Saint Jean*, pp. 362–3.

More specific evidence is, in fact, close at hand. In v. 18 the Evangelist cites Psalm 41:10b: 'He who ate my bread has lifted his heel against me.' The Greek translation of the first part of the Psalm ('He who ate my bread') reads *ho esthiôn artous mou*.[44] However, John has not used the same verb. He acknowledges that the passage comes from Scripture, but renders the text as: *ho trôgôn mou ton arton*. As can be seen, instead of the verb *esthiein*, the Evangelist uses *trôgein*.

There appears to have been a deliberate replacement of the usual, more 'proper' word for eating (*esthiein*), which is found in the Septuagint Greek of the Psalm. The verb used to replace it (*trôgein*) is a much less delicate term. It means 'to munch', or 'to crunch with the teeth'.[45] Once this is appreciated, it is most informative to see that John has used the same forceful and very physical verb of 'eating' on only three other occasions. He uses it to indicate unequivocally that he is referring to physical eating in the eucharistic passage of 6:51c–58:[46]

6:54. He who eats (*ho trôgôn*) my flesh and drinks my blood.
6:56. He who eats (*ho trôgôn*) my flesh and drinks my blood.
6:57. He who eats (*ho trôgôn*) me will live because of me.

The Fourth Evangelist has deliberately changed the verb in his citation of the Greek of the Psalm to link the gift of the morsel in 13:26, already prophesied by Jesus' use of Scripture in v. 18, with the most explicit eucharistic material in the Gospel: 6:51c–58.

The use of Psalm 41:10 may have been a part of the early Church's traditional explanation of what happened at the Last Supper, as Mark 14:18 also seems to make reference to it: 'One of you will betray me, one who is eating (*ho esthiôn*) with me.' Mark, however, has the more 'correct' verb for eating at table. Although he does not quote the Psalm, the same tradition could be behind Luke's

---

[44] The Greek Bible, used by the early Church, was called the Septuagint (indicated by the sigla LXX). Its numbering of the Psalms is different. In the Septuagint this passage is found at Ps. 40:10b.

[45] There has been some discussion on the significance of the two verbs in the late Greek of the New Testament. See, on this, C. Spicq, '*Trôgein*: Est-il synonyme de *phagein* et d'*esthiein* dans le Nouveau Testament?', *New Testament Studies* 26 (1979–80) 414–19. Spicq concludes: 'Until St John *trôgein* had never been used in a religious text. The Evangelist uses it to insist upon the real nature of the eating, all the while indicating that it was not a question of an impossible "man-eating"' (my translation).

[46] There has been much discussion for and against the eucharistic nature of John 6. But even those who would prefer to argue that the Fourth Gospel is a purely 'word' Gospel, without reference to the sacraments, find it impossible to explain away the clearly eucharistic themes of 6:51c–58. As such, they would generally relegate this passage to the hand of a later redactor. For a full discussion, with bibliographical references, see Moloney, *Johannine Son*, pp. 87–107.

words of Jesus at the Last Supper: 'Behold the hand of him who betrays me is with me on the table' (Luke 22:21).

John has *deliberately* re-fashioned this Old Testament passage, used by the early Church in close association with the Supper narrative. Thus his sharing of a morsel with Judas links 13:21–38 with the traditional accounts of the Last Supper, evidenced by the use of Psalm 41:10 in both Mark and Luke. But he has not simply developed this use of an Old Testament passage from the tradition. He has also used a verb (*trôgein*) linking the morsel he gave to Judas (vv. 18 and 26) with the flesh and blood of the Son of Man referred to in the clearest eucharistic material in the Gospel: the discourse by the lake of Tiberias (John 6:51c–58). These eucharistic hints should not be missed by John's readers.

In the light of this evidence, any doubt about v. 26b and the inclusion of words with close contacts with the celebration of the Eucharist can be resolved. The RSV reads: 'So when he had dipped the morsel, he gave it to Judas, the son of Simon Iscariot.' However, many ancient manuscripts read: 'So when he had dipped the morsel, *he took it* and gave it to Judas, the son of Simon Iscariot.' The inclusion of the reference to Jesus' taking the morsel (Greek *kai lambanei*) would recall Jesus' deliberate action of taking bread in the bread miracles in all four gospels (Mark 6:41; 8:6; Matt. 14:19; 15:36; Luke 9:16; John 6:11). As we have seen, all these passages are eucharistic. The same expression is found in the Synoptic reports of the Last Supper (Mark 14:22; Matt. 26:26; Luke 22:19; 1 Cor. 11:23).

Given the eucharistic hints involved in his use of the verb *trôgein* in the quotation from Psalm 41 in v. 18, I would further argue that the Evangelist originally wrote that Jesus 'takes' the morsel before giving it to Judas.[47] This expression should not be eliminated from the text as evidence of a scribal accommodation to other eucharistic passages.[48] It should be included because 13:26b is a eucharistic text. Although John is not depending upon the Synoptic tradition here, but telling his own story, he deliberately links this section on the gift of the morsel with eucharistic traditions that the Johannine community held in common with the early Church.[49]

---

[47] For detail, see Metzger, *A Textual Commentary on the Greek New Testament*, p. 241. The editors of the Greek New Testament thought that it should be included. See also, Schnackenburg, *St John*, vol. 3, p. 30.

[48] As many commentators would claim. See, for example, Barrett, *St John*, p. 447; Brown, *John*, p. 575; Haenchen, *John*, vol. 2, p. 113; and Lindars, *John*, p. 459.

[49] The Greek word used for 'morsel' (*psômion*) could refer to a morsel of either bread or meat. I am taking it for granted, along with most commentators, that bread is referred to here. See, however, Lagrange, *Saint Jean*, p. 362, who argues that it was meat.

We can now claim that there are sufficient indications in the text itself to argue that the background to the meal and the gift of the morsel and of the new commandment in vv. 21–38 is eucharistic, just as the background to the footwashing and the gift of example in vv. 1–17 was baptismal. The whole of 13:1–38 indicates that Jesus shows the quality of his love — a love that makes God known — by choosing, forming, sending out and nourishing his disciples of all times, drawing them into the rhythm of his own self-giving life and death. The Fourth Evangelist has made this point very clear within the context of a meal that is deliberately indicated as eucharistic. Jesus gives the morsel to the most despised character in the story: Judas!

As John wrote his Gospel at the end of the first century, he was well aware that disciples always have, and always will, fail Jesus, deny him and betray him. But this is precisely the point of his understanding of the God and Father of Jesus Christ. It is in the immensity of his never-failing love for such disciples that John shows Jesus as the revelation of a unique God among us.

It has long been suspected that the sacraments of Baptism and Eucharist may be hidden beneath the narrative of John 13. I am suggesting that behind the story of the footwashing (vv. 1–17) there is the call to disciples to recognise their Baptism summoning them to the ways of their Master (v. 16). The 'story' of Jesus' self-giving for them, acted out in the footwashing, calls them to recognise that they have been called 'to have part' in Jesus (v. 9), to be swept up into the same rhythm of self-giving love: 'I have given you an example, that you also should do as I have done to you' (v. 15). This is what is meant by: 'If you know these things, blessed are you if you do them' (v. 17).

However, matching the footwashing (vv. 1–17), the Evangelist has told the story of the gift of the morsel (vv. 21–38). The themes of betrayal and denial become more explicit (vv. 21–22, 27–30, 36–38). 'And it was night' (v. 30). Yet, because of the Fourth Evangelist's remarkable understanding of God as a Father who loves the world so much that he gave his only Son for its life (see 3:16–17), Judas' departure into the night to betray Jesus cannot lead to darkness. It begins a process that will eventually lead to Jesus' enthronement on the Cross (see 18:33, 36–37; 19:3, 5, 12–16, 19, 15–27, 38–42). It is as the crucified that Jesus is King, and it is as the one lifted up upon the Cross (3:14; 8:28; 12:32–33) that he achieves the greatest moment in his presence among us (see 4:34; 17:4; 19:30). There he reveals the glory of God (see 8:28; 12:28; 13:31–32).[50]

Because this is so, the account of the sharing of the table and the

---

[50] On this, see the fine study of de la Potterie, *Hour of Jesus*, pp. 21–181.

gift of the morsel sheds light in the darkness. Like the footwashing, this account looks for its meaning to Jesus' total gift of himself in love to 'his own' on the Cross. This loving self-giving thus leads easily into a commandment that is a further 'gift': 'A new commandment I give to you, that you love one another; even as I have loved you, that you also love one another' (v. 34). How are these Christians, at the end of the first century, to know and experience the way in which Jesus has loved them? Wherein do they find the model that stands at the basis of the new commandment (see also 15:12, 17)?

As they celebrate the presence of their absent Lord in the Eucharist (6:51c–58; 19:34),[51] they are to recall that night on which he gave the morsel unconditionally to the one who failed him most (Judas). The Johannine community at the Eucharist came to know and experience the remarkable love that Jesus had shown them. The new commandment of love (vv. 34–35) summons them to exercise their discipleship, in the midst of their difficulties and failure, making that love known: 'By this all will know that you are my disciples, if you have love for one another' (v. 35).

Conclusion

The eucharistic elements in John 13 are not the main features of the chapter. However, the story of the gift of the eucharistic morsel is central to the overall and larger message of the Johannine Jesus, who summoned the Church to a new quality of love (13:13–17, 34–35). He was able to do this because he gave himself in love to disciples who did not love him in anything like the same way. Indeed, he even gave himself to Judas!

Léon-Dufour has perceptively indicated that the eucharistic traditions of the earliest Church have been transmitted in two forms: the cultic form and the testamentary form.[52] In his analysis of the Johannine material, he writes of the whole of chapters 13–16 as avoiding the cultic form, but of containing within itself an important eucharistic witness in the testamentary form: 'The love Christians have for one another is the real symbol of Christ's presence in this world.'[53] I am suggesting that this same message, based in the prior and extraordinary revelation of the love of God in Jesus (13:18–20), can be traced through an analysis of the structure and theology of 13:1–38, where Jesus' gift of the morsel still has hints of the Johannine community's eucharistic cult.

---

[51] See above, pp. 77–8.

[52] Léon-Dufour, *Sharing*, pp. 82–95.

[53] Ibid. p. 252. See pp. 249–52 for his remarks on John 13–16.

This leads us back to a re-statement of a theme that we have been tracing throughout this book. The Fourth Evangelist would not have been able to tell his story in this way unless his own community and its celebration of the Eucharist had not already provided him with what I would now claim was a 'traditional' understanding of the presence of Jesus in the Eucharist. The Fourth Evangelist repeats and deepens what we have already discovered in Mark, Matthew and Luke: the Eucharist celebrates and proclaims the presence of Jesus to the broken. Even at the end of the first century, the theme of the eucharist as the presence of Jesus to the broken persists. As Sandra Schneiders has written: 'Jesus' action was subversive of the sinful structures in which not only Peter [and Judas], but all of us, have a vested interest.'[54]

---

[54] Schneiders, 'The Footwashing', p. 91. She wrote only of the footwashing. The same applies to the gift of the morsel, and thus I have added the parenthetic reference to Judas.

CHAPTER SIX

The Eucharist at Corinth

If we were to follow a strictly historical sequence, a study of Paul's discussion of the celebration of the Lord's Table at Corinth (1 Cor. 11:17–34) should have formed our first exegetical study. The situation described in Corinth is probably the earliest evidence of the actual practice of celebrating the Eucharist in the early Church. While there are accounts of such meals celebrated in the Jerusalem Church in the early chapters of the Acts of the Apostles (see Acts 2:42–47; 20:7–11; 27:33–36), these reports were written by Luke some time in the 80s of the first century.[1] Paul's discussion with his Corinthian converts represents a very real situation some time early in the 50s.[2]

Chronological considerations, on the basis of the probable antiquity of the Gospel or Pauline letter in which these eucharistic texts appear, are only partially useful. These texts, and particularly the words used at the Last Supper, came to the various authors from

---

[1] See Menoud, 'Acts . . . and the Eucharist', pp. 84–106.

[2] On these issues, see any good introduction to the New Testament. For example, W. G. Kümmel, *Introduction to the New Testament* (London: SCM Press, 1975) pp. 269–79.

traditions older than themselves.[3] The present study attempts to understand one aspect of the theological and pastoral point of view that was in the intention of the writer when he came to use these older traditions. Our interest has been fixed throughout on those to whom the eucharistic Jesus is present.

For the purposes of our study, it has been helpful to look first at the broader canvas of the Gospel narratives in close association with one another. There the recipients have consistently been the disciples. Although the gospels are directed to Christian communities in the early Church, the 'story' has been about Jesus and his presence to his disciples. In Paul, we are able to focus our attention on 1 Corinthians 10–11, where Paul writes to his troublesome Corinthian converts about taking part in both the Table of the Lord and the feasts that were part of pagan cult (10:14–22), and about a form of eucharistic celebration where those who had nothing were humiliated (11:17–34).[4]

Paul's attention is directed primarily towards some extraordinary new Christians, who were having difficulty in living the Christian life they had accepted. The Apostle's only reference to Jesus' original loving gift of himself is found in the reported words of Jesus himself in 11:24: 'This is my body which is for you.' Although 1 Corinthians 10–11 does not have a narrative setting that illuminates Jesus' gift of himself to his disciples in the Eucharist, it is presupposed throughout. Paul's concern with the abuses that have crept into the Corinthians' celebrations of the Lord's Supper will lead him back to the foundation of the whole of his life and preaching: the saving death of Jesus.

In the gospels we found there was a need to range widely: the bread miracles (Mark and Matthew), the Last Supper narratives (Mark, Matthew and Luke), the journey to Emmaus (Luke), the footwashing and the gift of the morsel (John). With Paul, we have a 'test case' from the early Church. Our study of the Gospel narratives has shown that there was a pervading interest in Jesus' eucharistic presence to a sinful, broken Church, even though this message has been communicated in a variety of ways. In each case, however, the disciples represent the sinful, broken Church.

---

[3] For a recent attempt to trace the history of the development of the traditions from the event of Jesus down to the narratives as we find them in the New Testament, see Léon-Dufour, *Sharing*, pp. 157–79.

[4] It should be remembered that the written documents of the New Testament are only part of the reflection of the early Church. This is also the case with Paul. We are able to see some aspects of the Pauline understanding of the Eucharist because he had to address abuses in Corinth. This Pauline intervention may not give us a complete picture of Paul's eucharistic thought.

We must now ask whether Paul's instructions to his Corinthian converts are consistent with this message. This question is crucial, as 1 Corinthians 11:27–28 has often been quoted against the line of argument I have pursued through my analysis of the Gospel texts.[5] Indeed, the passage, lifted from its historical and literary context within Paul's argument in 1 Corinthians, reads strongly:

> Whoever therefore eats the bread or drinks the cup of the Lord in an unworthy manner will be guilty of profaning the body and blood of the Lord. Let a man examine himself and so eat of the bread and drink of the cup. (1 Cor. 11:27–28)

Over the centuries this passage has probably been the cause of the gradual 'distortion' of the New Testament message on the presence of the eucharistic Jesus to the broken. Indeed, the beginnings of a line of thought that presents the Eucharist for 'the worthy', on the basis of this text alone, can already be found in Augustine.[6] 1 Corinthians 11:27–28 has regularly been used in the traditional moral and dogmatic theology manuals as a biblical word *against* the presence of the broken and the sinful at the eucharistic table.[7]

A widespread traditional use of this passage from Paul would suggest that here we might find another approach to the eucharistic meal that also comes to us from the teaching and practice of the early Church. Perhaps the conclusions that our reading of the gospels have suggested represent one point of view among several, and should be read in terms of a parallel practice of 'exclusion' from the table, which, the tradition suggests, is to be found in 1 Corinthians 11.

---

[5] See, for example, the letter from Fr J. Ware, published in the *Advocate*, Thursday, 21 July 1988, p. 2, where he asks that this passage be considered when discussing this matter. Fr Ware referred to 1 Cor. 11:26–27. I assume that he would also include v. 28: 'Let a man examine himself.'

[6] Augustine, *Homilies on the Gospel of John*, Tractate LXII, 1 (Schaff, *Nicene and Post-Nicene Fathers*, First Series, vol. 7, p. 313).

[7] It is extremely interesting to consult the best of these manuals. See, for example, I. A. de Aldama, F. A. P. Solá Severino Gonzales & J. F. Sagüés, *Sacrae Theologiae Summa* (Biblioteca de Auctores Cristianos II/73; Madrid: La Editorial Catolica, 1953) pp. 280–1. The author of this section (de Aldama) is modest in his claims, and is well aware of difficulties created by reading the passage within the overall context. However, the traditional argument is made. A similar care is shown by H. Davis, *Moral and Pastoral Theology* (Heythrop Series 11; London: Sheed & Ward, 1959) vol. 3, pp. 101–2. After indicating the usual norms on the need for holiness in approaching the Eucharist, the author concludes: 'The obligation of confessing conscious unforgiven mortal sin before celebrating Mass or receiving Holy Communion is probably an obligation of Ecclesiastical law' (p. 101). In a note, Davis refers explicitly to 1 Cor. 11:28, concluding that it 'does not clearly prove the existence of a divine precept' (p. 101, note 1).

Given this possibility, it is pedagogically more satisfactory to present my analysis of this famous Pauline text as a conclusion, rather than as an introduction to this study. It is a conclusion that uses the Word of God as a control of all that I have claimed so far. Again we find ourselves searching for the authentic biblical message behind the Pauline understanding of the celebration of the Eucharist at Corinth. As we read the Word of God in the tradition, we must allow the Word of God to question the distortions that may have taken place in the tradition.[8] This question is particularly relevant in our study of 1 Corinthians 11:27–28.

The Context

As with our studies of the gospels, we must also situate Paul's use of material referring to, or linked with, the Corinthian Church's celebration of the Lord's Table within its overall literary and theological context. Throughout 1 Corinthians, Paul addresses problems that have arisen in the community at Corinth. There are divisions in the community (chapters 1–4, see 1:11), misuse of the body that does not respect its Christian importance (5:1–6:20), problems concerning sexual relations in marriage (7:1–9), divorce (7:10–16), changes in social and sexual status (7:17–40). Living in a pagan world, the Corinthian Christians have divided opinions about which food one should or should not eat (chapters 8–9). Some are over-confident in their abilities to judge what is of value or not in joining pagan cultic celebrations, and thus they are offending the scruples of the weak (10:1–11:1).

In chapters 11–14 Paul addresses a series of divisive problems that were arising within the Corinthians' liturgical assemblies: dress (11:2–16), the Lord's Supper (vv. 17–34) and the use and abuse of the gifts of the Spirit (chapters 12–14). Paul finally looks to the problem of the resurrection of the body, also apparently causing difficulties in this early Christian community (see 15:1–2). In each of these cases Paul discusses the very real problems of a church's enthusiastic beginnings.

Although Paul moves from one problem to another, and deals with each one in turn, through all the various issues that are dealt with from 1 Corinthians 8–14, a common theme can be traced. There are some who see themselves as specially gifted in their new-found religion. This leads them to adopt an attitude of superiority. Some tend to despise, belittle, override, or ridicule the others. Paul's reaction to this false enthusiasm is to protect the people who are treated as inferior.[9]

---

[8] See above, pp. 9–16.

[9] See Barth, *Rediscovering the Lord's Supper*, p. 65.

Throughout chapter 8 Paul deals with the question of eating food that has been sacrificed to idols. The problem is that there are some Corinthian Christians who are strong in faith and rich in knowledge, and they are quite content to go ahead and eat such meat. They correctly claim that idols are meaningless. Paul asks these 'strong people' that they renounce the liberty that their faith and knowledge have given them. Christ died for 'the weak', thus they must be respected and cared for. To offend them through eating meat that had been produced by a ritual slaughtering would be to offend Christ (see 8:11–12).

Paul presents himself as an example to the Corinthians in chapter 9. He has been given great privileges and gifts by God, who has called him to be an Apostle, but it would be better for Paul to die rather than insist upon privilege. His role is to take the part of the weak, to be a servant: 'To the weak I became weak, that I might win the weak' (9:22). He uses the image of himself as a long-distance runner, not punishing others to attain the victory, but punishing himself (vv. 24–27). This is the Pauline paradigm for the protection and care of the so-called 'inferior'.

The question of those who regard themselves as spiritually superior, sharing in food sacrificed to idols, is still in Paul's mind. He begins chapter 10 with a reminder to the Corinthians of what happened to Israel, despite its many privileges as God's people (vv. 1–13). Paul then turns to the specific issue of idol-worship. The 'strong' seem to see no problem, in their new-found freedom, in taking part in meals that were associated with pagan sacrifices. The 'strong' rightly regard such sacrifices as senseless. However, such an approach pays no attention to the 'weak'. God is praised by conduct that builds up the whole body, not by the arrogant assertion of one's own strength and knowledge of what is right or wrong (see 10:31–33).

Having dealt with problems that arise over the sharing in the assemblies and the table of the pagans, Paul now turns to the community's own assemblies and the Lord's Table. One of the more remarkable features of the newness of Christianity was the place of women in the life and worship of the Church.[10] Paul himself, with reference to a restoration of the original creative plan of God, has declared:

> For as many of you as were baptized into Christ have put on Christ. There is neither Jew nor Greek, there is neither slave nor free, *there is neither male nor female*; for you are all one in Christ Jesus.[11]

---

[10] See Moloney, *Woman*.

[11] For an excellent study of this passage, see B. Byrne, *Paul and the Christian· Woman* (Homebush: St Paul Publications, 1988) pp. 1–14.

But is it permissible that this should lead some to demonstrate their new-found emancipation by adopting a 'manly' pose in the assembly? Paul does not minimise the right of women to pray and prophesy, but he demands that it be done with humility and decency. Women must remain women (11:2–16).[12] As we will see, a similar concern for unity and right order is at the heart of 11:17–34, where the eucharistic words of Jesus himself will be called upon to remind the wealthy that Jesus died for all (vv. 23–25). To celebrate Eucharist in an arrogant and superior fashion that discriminated against the poor and the weak would be a denial of all that was Christian in the celebration.

The same basic problems lie behind the discussions of chapters 12–14, where some more charismatically gifted people seem to be claiming superiority. While there are many gifts, they should never divide the believers. The community must be marked by the quality of its love, not its division into the more and less gifted (chapter 13). The basic reason for this strange 'enthusiastic' form of Christianity is found in chapter 15. The Corinthians need to be reminded of the central place of Jesus' death and resurrection. They do not yet live the risen life. That is still to come.

The Corinthian community is obviously polarised. Although some scholars have attempted to unite all of these divisions around one common group, which opposed the Pauline vision,[13] there were probably many factions, each one living a new-found freedom in its own way. The two occasions in the Letter to the Corinthians where Paul makes reference to the community's eucharistic celebrations both appear within this context of hurtful division, which needs to be overcome. It is to a divided community that Paul writes. The factions cannot agree over their approach to idol-worship, their freedom to behave as they like at community services, and their use of charismatic gifts. Within this context Paul presents the eucharistic table as a place of union, summoning believers to 'remember' the story of Jesus' gift of himself for them.[14] How, asks Paul, can the Corinthian community, which was founded upon the preaching of the cross and resurrection (1 Cor. 11:23–25; 15:3–8), and which

---

[12] On this difficult passage, see again the illuminating and comprehensive study of Byrne, *Paul*, pp. 31–58.

[13] Especially W. Schmithals, *Gnosticism in Corinth: An Investigation of the Letters to the Corinthians* (Nashville/New York: Abingdon Press, 1971). For a good survey, see C. K. Barrett, *The Second Epistle to the Corinthians* (Black's New Testament Commentaries; London: A. & C. Black, 1973) pp. 36–50.

[14] For a good presentation of the divided community, see J. Murphy-O'Connor, 'Eucharist and Community in First Corinthians', *Worship* 50 (1976) 370–2 and 51 (1977) 64–9.

'remembers' that cross at its Eucharists, be divided between the 'strong' and the 'weak', the 'haves' and the 'have-nots'?

Our 'old man' had been crucified with Christ in the experience of the death of Baptism (see Rom. 6:3–6; Gal. 2:19), but the symbol of the Cross that Paul raises up over against the 'old world' has its roots in the bloody reality of the experience of Jesus. Are the Corinthians prepared to live that reality in their lives? This called for respect for the weak, for whom Christ died (1 Cor. 8:11, chapters 8–10), a welcome to all at the eucharistic table (11:27–34). They had to understand that no matter what gifts had been given, all were one (chapter 12), called to a remarkable quality of love (chapter 13), so that the quality of their Christianity would bring outsiders to faith (chapter 14).

1 Corinthians 10:14–22

As we have seen, 1 Corinthians 8–10 deals throughout with problems that arose among the Corinthian believers because they lived their Christian lives within a pagan environment.[15] The dangers of injuring the weak through an insensitive use of superior knowledge and understanding in eating meat sacrificed to idols were dealt with in 8:1–13. Although 9:1–27 concentrates on the experience of Paul himself, it is used as an example for the community (see especially vv. 19–22). Paul often uses this method. It is pointless only to preach. The preached word must be seen as a lived reality in the life of the preacher. Paul has no hesitation in telling the Corinthians: 'Be imitators of me, as I am of Christ' (11:1; see also 4:16–17; 1 Thess. 1:6; Gal. 1:16, 24; 4:12; Phil. 4:9).[16]

In an introductory passage, Paul deals with the terrible results of the over-confidence of the fathers of Israel (10:1–13). He is warning the Corinthians that there is a parallel between the situation of the chosen people, the Israelites in the desert, and that of the 'strong' in Corinth. Indeed, writing to a Christian community he claims that the Israelites ate a 'spiritual food' and drank a 'spiritual drink' from a 'spiritual Rock'. And the Rock was Christ (vv. 2–4).[17] Paul is drawing a close parallel between the experience of Israel, which passed through the waters of a baptism in its passage through the

---

[15] Many scholars have argued that 10:1–22 do not belong to this context. For a good survey, and a defence of the logic of Paul's argument, see G. Bornkamm, 'Lord's Supper and Church in Paul', in *Early Christian Experience* (London: SCM Press, 1969) pp. 123–5, 152–4. See also W. L. Willis, *Idol Meat in Corinth: The Pauline Argument in 1 Corinthians 8 and 10* (SBL Dissertation Series 68; Chico: Scholars Press, 1985) pp. 268–75.

[16] On this, see J. Murphy-O'Connor, *Becoming Human Together: The Pastoral Anthropology of St Paul* (Good News Studies 2; Wilmington: Michael Glazier, 1982) pp. 141–53.

[17] The RSV mistakenly translates the Greek as 'supernatural' food and drink.

sea (vv. 1–2), to be nourished by a spiritual food and drink from the Rock that was Christ (vv. 3–4). Israel had been supplied by God with a privileged participation in the benefits of Christ.[18] Despite this privilege, Israel fell. Thus, warns Paul: 'Let anyone who thinks that he stands take heed lest he fall' (v. 12).

Having already insinuated baptismal and eucharistic ideas into his argument, Paul returns to the question of the pagan rituals, and eating within those contexts. Although he seems to be jumping from one point to another, Paul is arguing the same case throughout: the threat that the 'strong' pose to the community as a whole when they rightly insist that 'an idol has no real existence' (8:4). Thus, while the claim of the 'strong' that the idol has no existence (see 8:4) is a perfectly valid slogan, Paul still insists that the Corinthians are to 'shun the worship of idols' (10:14). After his presentation of himself as a positive model (chapter 9) and the experience of Israel as a warning (10:1–13), he is once again appealing to the 'strong'.

Paul conducts his argument here by first establishing some essential common ground between himself and the 'strong'. To do this, he raises two rhetorical questions beginning with the expression 'is it not' (v. 16). Such a question (formed by the Greek *ouki estin*) expects a positive answer.[19] He takes it for granted that the Corinthians will assent to the truth that the cup and the bread that they share in the Eucharist is to be identified with Christ:

> The cup of blessing that we bless, is it not a common union [Greek *koinônia*] in the blood of Christ? The bread that we break, is it not a common union [*koinônia*] in the body of Christ? (10:16: *my translation*)

The RSV translates *koinônia* as 'participation', but this does not catch the power of the original Greek. It would be best translated as 'communion', which indicates the depth and mutuality of the sharing involved, but that could lead to confusion. We Christians often speak of 'communion' as the practice of receiving the species at the Eucharist. Thus I have used the rather clumsy but clear expression 'common union'. Paul shows immediately, in v. 17, that he wants to say more than the union that happens between Christ and the believer implied by our traditional use of the term 'communion'.

Having established that the wine and the bread create a union,

---

[18] On this, see C. K. Barrett, *The First Epistle to the Corinthians*, (Black's New Testament Commentaries; London: A. & C. Black, 1971) pp. 218–29.

[19] F. Blass, A. Debrunner & R. W. Funk, *A Greek Grammar of the New Testament and Other Early Christian Literature* (Chicago: University of Chicago Press, 1961) p. 220 (para. 427): 'Both *ou* and *mê* are still used in questions as in classical . . . often *ouki* when an affirmative answer is expected, *me* . . . when a negative one is expected.'

Paul then argues that the union takes place at two levels: 'Because there is one bread, we who are many are one body, for we all partake of the same loaf' (v. 17). It is not only that the person sharing the cup and the broken bread establishes a union with Christ. A further union is established through the 'partaking' (Greek *metechein*) of the same loaf: the union between all the members of the celebrating community.[20]

Through sharing in the body and blood of Christ, believers are united with him *and* with each other. The physical gesture of eating and drinking at the Christian sacred meal has the effect of bringing into being a new Body which is the physical presence of Christ in the world (see 6:15; 8:12; 12:12–27). All are united with Christ through faith and baptism (Gal. 3:26–28). The physical gesture of eating and drinking adds a new dimension. Since all share in the one drink which is Christ and in the one bread which is Christ, Christ (to put it very crudely) becomes a possession which all hold in common, and are thereby forged into unity.[21]

Although Paul uses his eucharistic traditions as part of another argument and not as an end in itself, he provides, in passing, his understanding of the eucharistic meal. The Eucharist is food for 'the body'. This means that the celebration of the Eucharist maintains and strengthens the union between the believers and Christ, and that they become, together, the community that belongs to him.[22]

Paul and the 'strong' have points of agreement in their understanding of the Eucharist. Thus vv. 16–17 state a belief that was common to all at Corinth. He can now call these same people to task. Recalling the practice of sharing the food offered as sacrifice in Israel, he reminds the 'strong' of the common union (*koinônia*), which the people offering the sacrifice had with the altar (v. 18). So it is with any food offered, even to the imaginary and worthless pagan idols (vv. 19–20). This enables Paul to make his central point:

---

[20] For a precise study of the meaning of *koinônia* here, see Léon-Dufour, *Sharing*, pp. 209–11 and J. Murphy-O'Connor, 'Eucharist and Community in First Corinthians', *Worship* 51 (1977) 58–9. For a concise but more wide-ranging study of the background to the term, see Willis, *Idol Meat*, pp. 167–81. On its use in vv. 16–17, see pp. 200–12. The term *metechein* is used by Paul as equivalent to *koinônein*. On this, see Ibid., pp. 196–7.

[21] J. Murphy-O'Connor, *1 Corinthians* (New Testament Message 10; Wilmington: Michael Glazier, 1979) p. 97. See also Léon-Dufour, *Sharing*, pp. 211–13.

[22] Barth, *Rediscovering the Lord's Supper*, pp. 33–42 argues strongly against this case. The key to his argument lies in his claim that v. 17a should be read as a Christological declaration: 'There is one bread' (Jesus Christ). His whole argument is somewhat forced, and distorts the obvious flow of Paul's argument in 10:14–22.

the act of taking part in a cultic meal established a close connection between the guests themselves and the power to which the victims had been offered (v. 21).

Paul clarifies for the Corinthians what *koinōnia*, participation in the body and blood of Christ, means from their own familiar experience of their pagan past and their pagan environment. He does not do this to say something new to them, but plainly to convince and win them over by something long familiar.[23]

In strictly objective terms, the 'strong' are theoretically correct. Paul has no intention of claiming that sacrificed food or pagan idols have any value whatsoever (v. 19). However, as they have agreed with Paul concerning their eucharistic celebrations (vv. 16–17), and as they know from Israel's tradition of sacrificing at the altar (v. 18), ritual gestures have both a vertical and a horizontal implication.

Paul insists that Christians who shared in the meals celebrated in pagan temples, in conjunction with the pagan sacrifices, were joining in more than a cheap meal! It was not only the food that was consumed. The horizontal 'common union', which was generated by the shared table, had to be considered. They joined themselves with pagans who *did* believe that idols had a real existence, and in this way the naïve Christians, in their supposed strength and knowledge, became 'partners with demons' (v. 20).

In vv. 21–22 Paul returns to the central importance of the 'common union', which was created between Christ and the believer, and the community of believers who shared at the eucharistic table. To share in the cup and the table of the demons, no matter what the 'strong' may have thought they were doing *subjectively*, was a public rupture between themselves and the rest of the community. Thus it was to destroy the *objective* union created at the Table of the Lord, sharing his cup and his bread. The 'strong' are thus told that it is impossible to participate at both the pagan tables and the Table of the Lord. As has already been shown by the experience of Israel (vv. 1–13), one must not understand the Christian sacraments of Baptism and Eucharist as securing the believer from all possible danger of contamination.

Paul closes his reflection by a sharp reminder of the ultimate authority of the Lord: 'Shall we provoke the Lord to jealousy? Are we stronger than he?' (v. 21). In this way he again looks back to his warning descriptions of what happened to an arrogant Israel, which prided itself in its privileges. 'With most of them God was not

---

[23] Bornkamm, 'Lord's Supper', p. 127.

pleased' (v. 5, see vv. 1–13).[24] To threaten the common union established by the Lord between himself and his community, and within the community itself, by an arrogant exercising of one's privileged understanding and knowledge is unacceptable — and dangerous.

Paul calls upon a basic belief, which he shared with his Corinthian converts. No matter what their variations on the way they thought the Christian life should be lived, Paul was able to *remind* them that at the Table of the Lord they established a union with Christ and a union among themselves.[25] 'In it we receive the body of Christ and, by receiving it, are and show ourselves to be the body of Christ.'[26] Sharing other meals, thinking themselves superior to any contamination from such nonsense as idols, demons and sacrificed foods, the Corinthians broke the union essential for the life of the body.

Paul uses the Corinthian community's celebration of the Eucharist to prove his point. Unlike the Gospel accounts that we have analysed, he is not 'instructing' his community on the place and significance of its eucharistic celebrations. He takes that instruction for granted. On the basis of the Corinthians' understanding of what happens at the eucharistic table, he is able to 'instruct' them on the need to avoid their ritual associations with pagans. The basis of their understanding is their double *koinônia*: their common union with Christ, and their common union with one another. In 11:17–34 Paul again recalls their celebration of the Eucharist because this *koinônia* was being seriously threatened.

1 Corinthians 11:17–34

If the Corinthian believers were theoretically in agreement that the cup of blessing that they blessed and the bread that they broke established a *koinônia* between the Lord and themselves and a *koinônia* that was the community (10:14–22), the actual celebration of the Lord's Table should have been marked by the 'common union' at the level of life. It appears that such was not the case (11:17–34).

---

[24] On the importance of vv. 1–13 for Paul's overall argument, see Willis, *Idol Meat*, pp. 123–63.

[25] It is useful to notice that Paul uses this same 'reminding' technique in both 11:23 concerning what they had learnt from him about the Eucharist and in 15:1–3a concerning what they had learnt from him about the resurrection.

[26] Bornkamm, 'Lord's Supper', p. 144. See also G. Theissen, 'Social Integration and Sacramental Activity: An Analysis of 1 Cor. 11:17–34', in *The Social Setting of Pauline Christianity: Essays on Corinth* (Philadelphia: Fortress Press, 1982) pp. 165–6.

Paul's discussion of the Corinthians' problematic participation in the Lord's Supper is approached in the following fashion. He first attacks the nature of their abuse of the eucharistic table in 11:17–22. This is followed by the Pauline version of the eucharistic words, with an additional exhortation, which comes from his own pen (vv. 23–26). Having told of Jesus' meal with his disciples, Paul then moves to his more theological conclusions and recommendations (vv. 27–34).

The passage must be read as a part of the overall argument of 1 Corinthians, and then within the context of chapters 8–14, which are dedicated to the protection and affirmation of the importance of the 'weaker' members of the community. What Paul has to say about the *koinônia* created at the table in 10:16–17 serves as an immediate preparation for 11:17–34. Only when these 'contexts' have been considered can we analyse the harsh words of vv. 27–28.

What do these words mean *within their proper Pauline context*? The Greek expression translated 'whoever, therefore, eats' (*hôste hos an esthiêi*) of v. 27 demands that the passage be interpreted in the light of what Paul has just written.[27] Although 1 Corinthians 11:27–28 has become a *locus classicus* in traditional discussions of who should be allowed to approach the eucharistic table, its Pauline setting is insufficiently considered. Our traditional reading of vv. 27–28, devoting no attention to Paul's overall argument, especially the details of the Corinthians' behaviour indicated in vv. 17–22, uses the warning to distance 'sinners', in *our* understanding of that term, from the eucharistic celebration. Such an approach to the passage is faulty: we must read and understand this important text in Paul's terms.

What was the 'unworthy manner' mentioned in v. 27? Why must a man 'examine himself' (v. 28)? The wider context of the passage under consideration provides the solution to these questions. It is found in Paul's attack on the Corinthian abuses in vv. 17–22, which are part of the wider problem of serious division in the community. Paul has been tackling these abuses throughout 1 Cor. 8–14. Here he expresses his displeasure over the divisions between 'those who have' and 'those who have not', which seem to have developed since Paul had been with the community: 'I hear that there are divisions among you' (v. 18). These divisions are described as follows: 'In eating, each one goes ahead with his own meal, and one is hungry and another is drunk. What! Do you not have houses to eat and drink in? Or do you despise the Church of God and humiliate those who have nothing? What shall I say to you? Shall I

---

[27] L. Dequeker & W. Zuidema, 'The Eucharist and St Paul: 1 Cor. 11:17–34', *Concilium* 4 (1968) 28 (the whole article: pp. 26–31).

commend you in this? No I shall not' (vv. 21–22).

The Lord's Supper was supposed to be a common meal,[28] but Paul has heard that this has become impossible at Corinth because such divisions between the wealthy and the humble had arisen that no one was concerned about the other.[29] Paul indicates that there are some people who simply do not have enough to eat (v. 22), while there are others who own their own private home where they could enjoy their wealth without creating divisions at the Table of the Lord (vv. 22, 34).[30] It would be better for the wealthy Corinthians to do such lavish eating in their own houses, rather than pretend a unity that their behaviour belies. Their behaviour, in addition to humiliating the have-nots, shows that they hold true community in contempt.[31]

This is the 'unworthy manner' of participating in the Eucharist chastised by Paul in the much-abused passage in v. 27, and the reason for the request that a man should 'examine himself' expressed in v. 28. The situation has been well summarised by C. K. Barrett:

> The rich man's actions are not controlled by love; they therefore amount to contempt not only of the poor, but also of God, who has called into his church not many wise, not many mighty, not many noble born (1:26). God has accepted the poor man, as he has accepted the man who is weak in faith and conscience (8:9–13; 10:29 f; Rom. 14:1, 3 f, 10, 13, 15:1, 7); the stronger (whether in human resources or in faith) must accept him too. It is by failure here that the Corinthians profane the sacramental aspect of the supper — not by litur-

---

[28] Bornkamm, 'Lord's Supper', pp. 134–8, argues that the Pauline text indicates the practice of a common meal, which preceded the sacramental action. Paul is attacking the abuse of that prior meal. Among others, Theissen, 'Social Integration', pp. 151–3, claims that it is now impossible to determine the organisation of the meal itself. The crucial elements were the breaking of bread and the giving of a cup in the name of the Lord.

[29] The exact nature of the division is discussed. Whether the wealthier people were *not sharing*, or *not waiting* for the less privileged. The discussion hinges upon the meaning of *prolambanei* ('takes before others have theirs' or 'going ahead with eating'?) in v. 21. The idea of 'waiting' is supported by the imperative 'wait for one another' (*allêlous ekdechesthe*) in v. 33. Whichever meaning one takes, the basic social point is the same: the poor were disadvantaged. For the discussion, see Barrett, pp. 262 & 276.

[30] Theissen, 'Social Integration', pp. 150–1. See also H. Conzelmann, *1 Corinthians: A Commentary on the First Epistle to the Corinthians* (Hermeneia; Philadelphia: Fortress Press, 1975) p. 195, note 26; Bornkamm, 'Lord's Supper', p. 126.

[31] See, on this, Murphy-O'Connor, *1 Corinthians*, pp. 110–11.

gical error, or by undervaluing it, but by prefixing it to an unbrotherly act.[32]

Although Paul may be seen as simply insisting on good order at the eucharistic meals, his complaint has a more profound motivation. As always, Paul turns to the saving death of Jesus Christ himself to ground his demands for Christian behaviour, in this case for unity at the Lord's Table. As the disunity is being created at the Table of the Lord, he recalls Jesus' own meal with his disciples.

Thus, after indicating that he is merely reminding the Corinthians of something that they already know, and which he himself had received (v. 23a),[33] Paul inserts his version of the eucharistic words of Jesus. As Paul reports them in 1 Corinthians (11:23–26), they are highlighted by the command, repeated over both the bread and the wine, to perform the action of breaking the bread and sharing the cup 'in remembrance of me' (vv. 24 and 25).[34] While this twice-repeated command would have had its origins in the earliest liturgies, it is not *only* a liturgical instruction.

As we have already seen in our consideration of the uniquely Matthean indication that the cup was Jesus' blood 'poured out for many for the forgiveness of sins' (Matt. 26:28), it is not enough to explain where the words came from. We must also ask: what is their significance in the particular context in which they are now found?[35] Paul is challenging his divided community to take seriously the words of Jesus: 'You do this in memory of me.' These words are not only a reminiscence of the liturgical practices of the earliest Church.

What must the Corinthian community do in remembrance of Jesus' broken body and shed blood? Paul's twofold use of this liturgical formula is an important challenge to the Corinthians to shed their petty divisions based on a distinction between those who have more and others who have less. These words are a summons to a deeper appreciation of their being caught up in the mystery of

---

[32] Barrett, *First Epistle*, pp. 263–4. For an interesting study of the social and theological background to these difficulties, see Theissen, 'Social Integration', pp. 145–74. See also Murphy-O'Connor, 'Eucharist and Community', pp. 64–9.

[33] Paul uses this ironic approach to his communities on several occasions. By repeating to them formulas that they already know and use, he is asking them to practise what they preach, to put their lives where their words are. As well as 1 Cor. 11:23–26, the same approach is particularly powerful in his recalling a hymn on Jesus' emptying himself unto death to the self-oriented Philippian community in Phil. 2:5–11.

[34] The Lucan version of the eucharistic words has the same command (see Luke 22:19). On this, see the excellent chapter in Léon-Dufour, *Sharing*, pp. 102–16.

[35] See above, pp. 50–1.

the obedient self-giving death of Jesus Christ for them (v. 24).[36] In celebrating Eucharist the Corinthians are caught up into the rhythm of that death 'for others'. The Lord's Table calls them to a deeper appreciation of the eucharistic nature of the Christian life.[37]

To celebrate Eucharist is to commit oneself to a discipleship that 'remembers' Jesus, not only in the breaking of the ritual bread and sharing the ritual cup, but also in 'imitation' of Jesus, in the ongoing breaking of one's own body and spilling of one's own blood 'in remembrance' of Jesus.[38] As Peter Henrici has recently written:

> When Jesus thus enjoins on his disciples the task of doing 'this' in his remembrance, all his activity is meant — not only his symbolic gesture at the Last Supper (which can and should be ritually repeated) but also his whole sacrificial attitude of delivering himself up to mankind in obedience to the Father.[39]

For this reason, Paul adds: 'You proclaim the Lord's death until he comes' (v. 26).[40] It is in the broken body and the spilt blood of a Church of disciples who *live* the Eucharist that they *celebrate* that the Lord's death is proclaimed in the world, until he comes again.[41] Paul

---

[36] This is particularly powerful if v. 24 is to be read as 'my body, broken for you'. In defence of this reading, see J. Duplacy, 'A propos d'un lieu variant', pp. 27–46.

[37] Léon-Dufour, *Sharing*, p. 113 puts it well: 'Here we have once again the three dimensions of memory: (1) by means of the present cultic action (2) we go back to the Jesus who at a point in history manifested and made real the presence of God the deliverer, and (3) who gives an everlasting salvation ... He is here, and I did not realize it! He is here, and so I open myself to the multitude of human beings.'

[38] For more detail on this perspective, see H. Kosmala, 'Das tut zu meinem Gedächtnis', *Novum Testamentum* 4 (1960) 81–94 and P. Henrici, '"Do this in remembrance of me": The sacrifice of Christ and the sacrifice of the faithful', *Communio: International Catholic Review* 12 (1985) 146–57. See the comprehensive study of F. Chenderlin, *'Do This as My Memorial'* (Analecta Biblica 99; Rome: Biblical Institute Press, 1982).

[39] Henrici, '"Do this in remembrance of me"', pp. 148–9. For a similar position from a dogmatic theologian, see K. Rahner, *The Practice of Faith: A Handbook of Contemporary Spirituality* (ed. Karl Lehmann & Albert Raffelt; New York: Crossroad, 1984) pp. 175–9. See, for example, p. 175: 'We can only receive the grace of Eucharist insofar as we personally also realize the sacrifice contained in it.'

[40] Against Barth, *Rediscovering the Lord's Supper*, pp. 42–4, I am reading v. 26, along with most commentators, as a Pauline comment on vv. 23–25, not as part of his eucharistic tradition. This does not mean, however, that the elements that form the comment were not, in themselves 'traditional'. See, on this, Conzelmann, *1 Corinthians*, pp. 201–2; Barrett, *First Epistle*, p. 270.

[41] For further consideration of this argument, with bibliography, see J. D. Laurance, 'The Eucharist as the Imitation of Christ', *Theological Studies* 47 (1986) 286–96. Especially useful is the survey of contemporary discussions on pp. 291–4. See also Bornkamm, 'Lord's Supper', pp. 140–1.

is telling his divided Corinthian community: 'You break your bodies and spill your blood, and in this way remember me.'[42] While remembering involves gratitude, it is above all an acceptance of the responsibility to prolong the saving mission of Christ.[43]

Thanks to this clarification made through the liturgy, the whole Christian life becomes an act of worship and proclamation: it 'proclaims the death of the Lord until he comes again' — that is, it makes clear the meaning and the source of the eschatological tension that gives shape to the Christian life (cf. 1 Cor. 7 and the letters to the Thessalonians).[44].

Looking back over the whole context of 1 Corinthians 11:17–34, we can see that Paul first calls for unity in vv. 17–22. However, the call to unity is not a call to unity for unity's sake. It is much more. It is a summons motivated by the need for the Corinthian believers 'to remember', to practise at the level of life what they proclaim at the level of ritual (vv. 23–26). '"To remember", in the New Testament, signified almost always to recall something or to think about it in such a way that it is expressed in speech or is formative for attitude and action.'[45]

Because Paul has now recalled the 'rhythm' of the self-giving life of Jesus, through the very words that the Corinthians themselves pronounce in their celebrations of the Eucharist, he is able to attack their divisions once more. To continue in their present practice would be to eat the bread and drink the cup 'unworthily' (v. 27). Thus they must examine themselves carefully on these issues before approaching the eucharistic meal (v. 28). This critical reading of 1 Corinthians 11:27–28 within the whole context of 11:17–34 warns us against its traditional use as a Pauline imperative giving

---

[42] I am not arguing that v. 26 is *only* about the eucharistic lifestyle of all who celebrate Eucharist. It is *also* that. See Léon-Dufour, *Sharing*, pp. 220–7. See also Kodell, *Eucharist*, p. 80: 'Scholars have become aware that both ideas may be contained in the call to remember: the Eucharist as a reminder to God and as a reminder to the followers of Jesus. God is reminded of his covenant promises in Jesus so that he will fulfil them, and the disciples are reminded of Jesus' self-gift in life and death so that they may imitate his example.' See also Jeremias, *Eucharistic Words*, pp. 237–55.

[43] See Murphy-O'Connor, 'Eucharist and Community', pp. 60–2.

[44] Henrici, '"Do this in remembrance of me"', p. 155. See also Laurance, 'The Eucharist as the Imitation of Christ', p. 289: 'Not only do truly Christian actions contain Christ in his saving events but . . . they do so because those same events somehow include in themselves the reality of all Christians living in this world.' See the further reflections of Martelet, *Risen Christ*, pp. 170–3.

[45] N. A. Dahl, 'Anamnesis: Memory and Commemoration in Early Christianity', in *Jesus in the Memory of the Early Church* (Minneapolis: Augsburg, 1976) p. 13 (the whole article: pp. 11–29). See pp. 21–4 on eucharistic memory, concluding: 'Early Christianity was not only faith and worship, but also a way of life' (p. 24).

the subsequent Church authority to separate the broken from the eucharistic table.[46]

In v. 29 Paul further instructs the Corinthians: 'Anyone who eats and drinks without discerning the body eats and drinks judgment upon himself.' This condemnation also needs to be carefully analysed. There is a division over the interpretation of the expression 'the body' in this passage. A traditional Catholic interpretation has seen it as not discerning the eucharistic presence,[47] while the favoured Protestant interpretation has been to see it as a reference to 'the body of Christ', the community as 'Church'.[48]

Probably both interpretations are involved. 'Not to discern the body' is to fail to recognise the Lord's presence in the Eucharist in the sense of the Lord who died for us (see v. 24: 'This is my body which is *huper humôn* [for you]'). It is not enough to see that the word 'body' refers to the presence of Jesus in the Sacrament. In the light of what Paul had already said to the Corinthians about 'the body' in 10:16–17, the context forces us to pay attention to the fact that Paul is particularly concerned that the Corinthians remember that the body of Jesus was given unto death, in obedience to the Father, in love for them, for all of them who form the one body, which is the Church![49]

Thus, a further meaning to 'the body' must be discerned. If the Corinthians ignore the context of the whole community in their eucharistic meals, they are failing to discern 'the body' that is

---

[46] There are still contemporary writers who continue with this uncritical use of 1 Cor. 11:27–28, without any reference to its literary and theological context. See, for example, E. Diederich, 'Reflections on Post-Conciliar Shifts in Eucharistic Faith and Practice', *Communio: International Theological Review* 12 (1985) 234 (the whole article: pp. 223–37). See also 'Propositions on the Doctrine of Christian Marriage', in M. Sharkey (ed.), *International Theological Commission: Texts and Documents 1969–1985* (San Francisco: Ignatius Press, 1989) p. 174. The whole document of the ITC (1977) is found on pp. 163–74.

[47] See, for example, A. Piolanti, *The Holy Eucharist* (New York: Desclée, 1961) pp. 45–6; P. Benoit, 'The Accounts of the Institution and What they Imply', in AA.VV, *The Eucharist in the New Testament: A Symposium* (London: Geoffrey Chapman, 1964) p. 93. A contemporary Catholic scholar, Murphy-O'Connor, *1 Corinthians*, p. 114, comments as follows: 'It is sometimes said that what Paul demands here is that participants distinguish the eucharist from common food, but this does not fit the context, and betrays a preoccupation with the doctrine of the real presence characteristic of a much later era.'

[48] See the discussion in Barrett, *First Epistle*, pp. 273–5. See also, Bornkamm, 'Lord's Supper', pp. 148–52.

[49] Against Theissen, 'Social Integration', pp. 148–9. Theissen argues that the words over the bread have a 'practical meaning': 'This bread is here for all of you.' The self-giving death of the historical Jesus is in Paul's mind, not the universal availability of the bread. Of course, the latter is a consequence of the former. See Kodell, *Eucharist*, pp. 78–81.

the community itself. They would be proclaiming the presence of the Lord in a way that ran counter to that very 'rhythm' of the offering of Christ that they claimed to be 'remembering' in their celebration.[50]

As we have just seen, the Christian is called to repeat the self-gift of Christ in his memory both in cult and in life. Not to celebrate Eucharist in this way is to 'eat and drink judgment' upon oneself (v. 29). By not recognising the sacrificed 'body' of Jesus in the Eucharist, one offends against the 'body' that is the Church, called to repeat that sacrifice in its own life.[51] As in 10:14–22, Paul is using the community's understanding and practice of the Eucharist to teach. To threaten the common union established by the Lord between himself and his community, and within the community itself, by an arrogant exercising of one's privileges, is unacceptable — and dangerous (vv. 30–31).[52]

Paul touches on one of the deepest of all mysteries, if indeed it be true that the paradox of human existence is to be found in the fact that human beings are at once individual persons and essentially social beings. Believers in Jesus become more fully themselves and more closely associated with their brothers and sisters, the more intimately united they are with their Savior.[53]

Conclusion

Our study of the Pauline references to the celebration of the Eucharist within the community at Corinth has attempted to place Paul's understanding of those celebrations as a challenge to a divided community to recall that 'Because there is one bread, we who are many are one body, for we all partake of the same loaf' (1 Cor.

---

[50] Rahner has appreciated this in his use of 1 Cor. 11:29. See Rahner, *Practice of Faith*, p. 178: 'The meaning of 1 Corinthians 11:29 will always remain true: by sins against the love of neighbor we eat and drink judgment for ourselves in the Lord's Supper.'

[51] For these reflections, I am in debt to a personal communication from Brendan Byrne, SJ. See also Dequeker & Zuidema, 'The Eucharist and St Paul', pp. 29–30, and C. Perrot, 'Lecture de 1 Co. 11:17–34', in AA.VV, *Le Corps*, p. 96: 'Among the Corinthians, it is not "the real presence" of their Lord which is difficult for them, but the Cross . . . and this theme sounds throughout the whole of the letter' (my translation).

[52] 1 Cor. 11:30 speaks of the weak, the sick and the dead in the community, and links this phenomenon to their poor use of the Lord's Table. This difficult verse indicates that the destructive powers of the old age, sickness and death, are still active. But it also means that they are sent to them from the Lord to execute his judgement. On the whole of vv. 30–34, see Bornkamm, 'Lord's Supper', p. 150.

[53] Léon-Dufour, *Sharing*, p. 229.

10:17). Unfortunately, the traditional use of 1 Cor. 11:27–28 has tended to ignore the overall context, both literary and historical, which has produced this passage.[54]

My analysis of the context of the Pauline teaching on the Eucharist that surrounds 1 Cor. 11:27–28 shows that this passage was originally written to accuse the Corinthian Christians of their sinfulness in so celebrating their eucharistic meals that some were excluded.

> It is eating unfittingly when the Supper of the *Lord* is treated as one's 'own supper'. Then one becomes 'guilty' inasmuch as the man who celebrates unfittingly sets himself alongside those who kill the Lord instead of proclaiming his death.[55]

This behaviour contradicted what was an 'agreed position', spelt out in 10:16–17. Thus, there was a 'lie' in the lives of the faithful: they were not proclaiming with their lives what they were celebrating in cult. There was a 'contradiction between an early Christian congregation's quarrels and its understanding of itself as an eschatological community of love'.[56] This could not be allowed in any genuine Christian community, and thus Paul is severe in his intervention.

The Corinthians could not claim to be 'the body of the Lord' (the Church) as long as they did not 'discern the body' (equally Church) in those lesser creatures, the poor, abandoned and unworthy, whom they were excluding from the eucharistic table.[57] Although we are here dealing with a 'literary form' different from the narrative texts that we considered in our studies of the four gospels, the underlying insistence of Jesus can still be sensed. The eucharistic table is not only for the privileged, and any attempt to make it so must be exposed and corrected.

---

[54] By the 'literary context' I mean all that comes before and after the passage, and the overall message and structure of 1 Corinthians as a literary document. By the 'historical context' I mean the situation in the life of these extraordinary early Christians which led Paul to 'remember' their eucharistic celebrations and the link with the death of Jesus, as he had taught them.

[55] Conzelmann, *1 Corinthians*, p. 201. See also W. F. Orr & J. A. Walther, *1 Corinthians* (Anchor Bible 32; New York: Doubleday, 1976) p. 274: 'Judgement comes because they do not discriminate the divine nature of this fellowship and are guilty of splitting it apart and mistreating its humbler members.'

[56] Theissen, 'Social Integration', p. 168.

[57] Barth, *Rediscovering the Lord's Supper*, p. 68: 'It is . . . absurd to prevent from sitting at the table any peson who is invited by Christ and desires to follow Christ's call. These very suspect or condemnable persons may be messengers of Christ.'

The 'lack of discerning' (see v. 29) that Paul would not allow in the Corinthian community should similarly not be allowed in any Christian community. As we have seen, his words to the Corinthians on this issue are stern: 'What shall I say to you? Shall I commend you in this? No I will not' (11:22). Paul's words should warn us lest we, in our arrogance, merit the same accusations as we develop and defend traditions that are aimed at excluding, rather than including, all who look to the eucharistic table as the place where they can meet the Lord, crucified for them (see 11:24).

The Church is called to recognise that it finds its very reason for existence in the needs of all who look to the Lord's Table for oneness with him, and for oneness in the community itself. Only then will it meet the Pauline requirements for a truly Christian Eucharist.[58] Circumstances and legislation that canonise division and exclusion need to come under scrutiny. They may merit for us the charge that Paul levelled at the Christian community in Corinth: 'When you meet together it is not the Lord's supper that you eat' (1 Cor. 11:20).

Paul tells the story of the night when Jesus was betrayed to remind the Corinthians that Jesus did not accept the suffering that was his destiny in some passive way. It was not something that was 'for himself'. Fully aware that he had been called to a radical loyalty to both God and to his fellow human beings, the experience of Calvary was embraced to produce fruits that would save the world. So must it also be for those who are caught up in the 'rhythm' of Eucharist, a rhythm that touches both celebration and life.

If we are truly following in the footsteps of Jesus we are to lead lives that are marked by a deep awareness that we are united to Jesus, to God and to the rest of humankind. Like Jesus, we too live eucharistic lives that both recall the saving events that took place in the life and death of Jesus, and which indicate that we too are prepared to be victims, breaking our bodies and spilling our blood for others. The eucharistic liturgy is the source and the summit of a eucharistic life given without limit (see *Sacrosanctum Concilium* 10). Such was the quality of the life of Jesus: it must mark the lives of all his disciples, as they live henceforth by and in him.

It is within this context that one can come more fully to appreciate what it means to celebrate the Eucharist:

> The eucharistic liturgy seems to complicate my life, since instead of simply devoting myself to my daily tasks I must set aside a little time for this occupation that seems useless but is in fact indispensable if I wish to bear witness to my Christian

---

[58] See also the remarks of Martelet, *Risen Christ*, pp. 37–9.

faith. The truth of this statement becomes inescapably clear once I look upon the Eucharist not as a 'means' of obtaining graces but as an exercise of my Christian language. If I am to exist fully, I must express myself in this way.[59]

The Eucharist is not a prayer wheel that we are able to spin every day, and a little more solemnly on Sundays. It is the 'language' of my life. It expresses more than anything else my being caught up into the saving mystery of the self-giving of Jesus in obedience and love unto death.

---

[59] Léon-Dufour, *Sharing*, p. 288. See the whole of pp. 283–9, upon which these last few paragraphs depend.

CHAPTER SEVEN

Clasping sinners to her bosom

*T*he New Testament witness to the life, teaching, death and resurrection of the person of Jesus of Nazareth has many faces. My analysis of how the various authors have used their own experience and understanding of the Eucharist is but one example of that fact. This is often difficult for contemporary Christians to grasp. In the light of the multiplicity of presentations of the celebration of the Eucharist, which can be traced through an analysis of the New Testament, and even of the various ways in which eucharistic words of Jesus himself appear, the question about what exactly happened at the beginnings of our eucharistic tradition inevitably arises.

This is an important question. Our Christian faith cannot be based totally on the faith of the early Church as it experienced and confessed the Risen Lord in its midst.[1] It must look back to its basis

---

[1] Rudolf Bultmann, the noted New Testament scholar, believed passionately that this was exactly what Christian faith should be. He claimed that one should have no interest in the pre-Easter Jesus. See, for the classical statements of this belief, R. Bultmann, 'New Testament and Mythology' [original German: 1941] in R. Bultmann, *New Testament and Mythology and Other Basic Writings* (selected, edited and translated by Schubert M. Ogden; Philadelphia: Fortress, 1984) and 'On the Problem of Demythologizing' [original German: 1952] in ibid. pp. 95–130.

in given historical data that come from the life, teaching, death and resurrection of the founder of Christianity, Jesus of Nazareth. It is equally important, however, to realise that it cannot be *only* that.[2] Christianity is a religion that is based on revealed truths.[3] While it must look back to the historical basis of all that it believes and attempts to live in the events of the life of Jesus himself, it must look beyond those few crucial years into its own history. The Spirit of Jesus lives on in the post-Easter communities, and this gives the whole of Christian history the possibility of being a place where God makes himself known. The early Church itself was aware of this truth. It was very clearly articulated in the teaching of the Johannine Jesus on the gift of the Paraclete:

> I have yet many things to say to you, but you cannot bear them now. When the Spirit of truth comes, he will guide you into all the truth; for he will not speak on his own authority, but whatever he hears he will speak, and he will declare to you the things that are to come. He will glorify me, for he will take what is mine and declare it to you. (John 16:12–14)[4]

The text of the New Testament is part of Christian history. Our first known documents (the Letters of Paul) date from about 50–64 CE. The gospels themselves did not begin to appear until about 70 CE. The Christian story was well under way before the documents that eventually came to form the New Testament began to appear. A New Testament was not officially recognised in the Church until some centuries later.[5]

Even though the New Testament is a product of Christian experience, it touches both 'what actually happened', and how the inspired Church eventually came to reflect on that data. Christianity looks back to the texts of the New Testament as an authoritative, inspired witness, which both opens our eyes to the 'fact' of Jesus of Nazareth and shows us the presence of the Spirit leading the Church to an authoritative interpretation of the 'significance' of those events.

---

[2] Another noted New Testament scholar, Joachim Jeremias, devoted his whole scholarly life to an attempt to develop a biblical theology based entirely on a historical reconstruction of the words and actions of the pre-Easter Jesus. See, J. Jeremias, *The Theology of the New Testament: The Proclamation of Jesus* (London: SCM Press, 1970).

[3] See above, pp. 9–14.

[4] See especially G. M. Burge, *The Anointed Community: The Holy Spirit in the Johannine Tradition* (Grand Rapids: Eerdmans, 1987) pp. 198–221.

[5] See, on this, Moloney, *Living Voice*, pp. 18–21.

Christian faith presupposes a historical event able to be traced through the texts from the New Testament. This is the case with a Last Supper, which Jesus shared with his fragile disciples. It became the first of many suppers that he has gone on sharing with his equally fragile Church over the centuries of Christian history. All versions of the eucharistic words of Jesus are marked by the word 'until' (Greek *heôs*):

> . . . *until* that day when I drink it new in the kingdom of God. (Mark 14:25)
> . . . *until* that day when I drink it new with you in my Father's kingdom. (Matt. 26:29)
> . . . *until* the kingdom of God comes. (Luke 22:18)
> You proclaim the Lord's death *until* (Greek: *achri hou*) he comes. (1 Cor. 11:26)

In the midst of betrayal, denial and the terror of an oncoming death, Jesus confidently speaks of his future presence to his disciples at a meal that will mark the reigning presence of God, his Father, among them. Paul adds the essential indication that the eucharistic presence of Jesus, in both Christian cult and Christian life, will last until Jesus' final return. This widely attested expression of the faith of the earliest Church was based on a foundational experience that took place on the night before Jesus died.[6]

But in the final analysis, faith is not based simply on an authentication of the event. Despite many who would like to be able to point to the 'facts' of the Jesus-story, and thus to the absolute truth of the Christian faith, it has not come down to us in that way. Indeed, this would reduce the Christian faith to an act of unaided reason calling into question the intellectual honesty of those who do not accept Christianity. It could not justifiably be called 'faith'. Christian faith has been inspired by the texts that have been transmitted by a community of witnesses. These witnesses speak through the texts, of Jesus Christ in whom they believe. Thus, we do not look simply to the events and words from the life of the Galilean whom any of his contemporaries might have met. The witness of the New Testament is the indispensable mediator of the event of Jesus who was exalted as Lord.[7]

On the basis of these considerations, our study of the New Testament raises two concluding questions.

---

[6] For a study of the authenticity of this aspect of the supper, attested across all the traditions, see Léon-Dufour, *Sharing*, pp. 165–8.

[7] See Léon-Dufour, *Sharing*, p. 158. The same affirmation could be made of tradition, but that would take us beyond the limitations of this study. See also Kodell, *Eucharist*, pp. 130–2.

1. Does the evidence of the Gospels and of Paul raise questions about the presence of 'the broken' at Jesus' own table?
2. Does the creative use of the eucharistic material by the various authors of the New Testament documents challenge the contemporary Christian Church in any way?

Jesus at Table with the Broken

This study has been concerned throughout to uncover the particular message of each of the New Testament authors who have left important and explicit teachings on the celebration of the Eucharist: Mark, Matthew, Luke, John and Paul.[8] A great deal of strictly historical research has been done to rediscover Jesus' actual celebration of a Last Supper with his disciples, and the eventual transmission of the continuation of a practice based on that meal through the early years of the Church's life. Such research is important, but highly speculative. Our study has not considered these historical questions. We have been uncovering a Marcan, Matthean, Lucan, Johannine and Pauline understanding of the Eucharist from an analysis of the documents *as we now have them*. As each Evangelist, or Paul, told the story of an event that took place in the 'then' of the life of Jesus, he has told it to challenge the 'now' of his own Christian community. As the Church reads and proclaims these texts, they continue to challenge the 'now' of contemporary eucharistic faith and practice.

A historical question must nevertheless be asked. Across the narratives we have traced a basic theme: the presence of Jesus to the broken. Although the Evangelists and Paul have necessarily used their eucharistic material in a variety of ways, they all have, somewhere in their message, a fundamental idea of the Eucharist as the presence of Jesus to the broken: the betrayers, the deniers, the frightened, the poor as well as the rich. Where did this notion come from? This is a particularly important question in the light of the subsequent Christian tradition that the Lord's Table is reserved for those worthy to approach it, those whom we consider to be without serious sin.

When studying the foundational documents of Christianity, the most obvious place to look for their inspiration is the person of Jesus of Nazareth. His story is told in order to communicate faith in him as the Christ and the Son of God (see Mark 1:1). Did Jesus share his table with others? Are there any indications of the people with whom he shared his table? How did his contemporaries react to his

---

[8] I am, of course, using the names Mark, Matthew, Luke and John in their traditional application to the gospels to which they have been attached. I have no intention to thus indicate historically certain authors in a twentieth-century sense of that word.

practice of meal-fellowship? The evidence of the New Testament is very consistent. We have already glanced at some of the Lucan material that deals with Jesus' sharing his table with sinners and outcasts,[9] but the evidence for such table-fellowship reaches wider than Luke's account.

According to the gospels, Jesus' contemporaries were staggered by his preparedness to share his own table with sinners (Mark 2:15; Luke 15:1–2), to deliberately visit the tables of tax-collectors (Luke 19:5) and to allow a prostitute to attend to him at a table where he was an invited guest (Luke 7:36–38). In these situations, his table-fellowship was most unsuitable for a religious leader or a rabbi. He was quite active in sharing his table with the irreligious. Some passages in the gospels give direct reports of such meals (see Mark 2:16–17; Matt. 11:19; Luke 15:1–2; 19:8), while others refer indirectly to Jesus' sharing of the table with sinners and irreligious people (Matt. 20:1–16; 21:28–32; Luke 7:41–43).

Not only do we have reports of Jesus' sharing both his own table and the table of others in this form of table-fellowship, but we also hear of the consternation and anger that this created among 'the righteous' (see Mark 2:16; Matt. 11:19; Luke 15:2; 19:7; see also Luke 15:25–32). As if this were not enough, the gospels also report that the broken, the sinful and 'the unrighteous' were both privileged and delighted to share such fellowship (Luke 19:9; Mark 2:19). Jesus' parables often return to this practice, speaking boldly of God's kingdom as a place where the accepted absolutes of religion, history and culture will be overturned, where the outcasts and the sinners will be welcomed at the table (Luke 14:12–24, 15:11–32; Matt. 8:11; 11:16–19).[10]

The gospels, therefore, agree that Jesus shared his table with sinners and outcasts, with the broken, and that he spoke boldly of such sharing as a sign of the inbreak of God's presence as king. However, how sure can we be that these narratives record an authentic memory of something that Jesus actually did and said? Are we in touch with an authentic practice of Jesus? Is it possible that the Evangelists themselves created this image of Jesus at table, gathering sinners around him from the highways and the byways? In the light of the motley crowd who eventually came to form their own communities, such stories and parables would give a basis to their preaching in the life of Jesus. He too admitted cultural outsiders to his community, and thus also to the eucharistic table. By placing

---

[9] See above, pp. 59–64.

[10] On this, see F. J. Moloney, 'Jesus Christ: The question to cultures', *Pacifica* 1 (1988) 18–21 (the whole article: pp. 15–43).

such an outrageous practice in the story of Jesus himself, the leaders of the early communities could advocate sharing the eucharistic table with Gentiles and sinners. This practice needed support, as many early Christians found it difficult to accept.

Over the past century, scholars have grappled with the difficult task of reaching behind the narratives as we now have them in the New Testament to discover the authentic memory of Jesus upon which these narratives are founded. There is no single version of what Jesus did beside the lake when he fed a multitude. Even more surprisingly, there is no single version of what he said and did on the night before he died, at his Last Supper. We are amazed that such an important event has not been firmly and definitively 'archived' somewhere so that it can be taken out, dusted off, and examined in its original state.

In order to 'look behind' the narratives to the historical Jesus, contemporary scholars have developed 'criteria' to approach the text. Many such criteria have been suggested, but the main ones are the criteria of dissimilarity, coherence and multiple attestation.[11] There are weaknesses and questionable presuppositions in these criteria,[12] but they are helpful guides in establishing some of the material that can certainly be claimed for the life and teaching of Jesus himself.

The criterion of dissimilarity can be defined as follows:

> The earliest form of a saying [a practice] which we can reach may be regarded as authentic if it can be shown to be dissimilar to characteristic emphases both of ancient Judaism and of the early Church, and will particularly be the case where Christian tradition oriented towards Judaism can be shown to have modified the saying [the practice] away from its original emphasis.[13]

The weakness of this criterion is obvious. It leaves Jesus completely out of any historical, cultural and religious context. His roots

---

[11] I am using the good summary of N. Perrin, *Rediscovering the Teaching of Jesus* (London: SCM Press, 1967), pp. 38–49. See also D. Abernathy, *Understanding the Teaching of Jesus: Based on the Lecture Series of Norman Perrin 'The Teaching of Jesus'* (New York: Seabury, 1983). A further 'criterion' perfected by Joachim Jeremias has been the identification of a possible Aramaic substratum to the Greek text. On this, see the summary of Perrin, *Rediscovering*, pp. 36–8. Of course, this may only take us back to an Aramaic stage of the tradition, and not necessarily to Jesus himself.

[12] For a serious criticism of them, see M. D. Hooker, 'Christology and Methodology', *New Testament Studies* 17 (1970–71) 480–7. See also the critical survey of R. S. Barbour, *Traditio-Historical Criticism of the Gospels* (Studies in Creative Criticism 4; London: SPCK, 1972).

[13] Perrin, *Rediscovering*, p. 39 (my parentheses).

were within Judaism, and the Church looked back to what he said and did for its own practices and teaching. The criterion of dissimilarity, applied ruthlessly, would leave us with a Jesus of Nazareth who lived in a vacuum. This was certainly not the case.[14] Useful though the criterion is, it must be applied with an awareness of Jesus' being a man of his place and times.

The early Church may have admitted to its ranks, and thus to its eucharistic table, people whom 'the establishment' would have excluded,[15] but, even so, the sense of a Christian community 'over against' the rest of the world eventually emerged (see, for example, 1 John).[16] This eventual tendency of the early communities, therefore, must be judged as 'dissimilar' from Jesus' teaching and practice.

Jesus' dissimilarity with traditional Judaism in his meal-fellowship is very obvious. Table-fellowship indicated the distinction between the clean and the unclean, the righteous and the sinners. Tax-collectors, prostitutes and sinners simply had to be shunned if one was truly to belong to Israel.[17] The narratives that tell of Jesus' sharing his life and his table with people from this social setting could not have been invented by the early Church. We find them in the New Testament because such table-fellowship was a regular part of Jesus' own life. 'This makes us realize the enormity of Jesus' act in calling a publican to be one of his intimate disciples (Matt. 9.9 par.; 10.3), and announcing the Good News to publicans and "sinners" by sitting down to eat with them.'[18]

The second criterion that has been developed, and which is widely used, the criterion of coherence, has been described as follows:

> Material from the earliest strata of the tradition may be accepted as authentic if it can be shown to cohere with

---

[14] See, for example, D. J. Harrington, 'The Jewishness of Jesus: Facing Some Problems', *Catholic Biblical Quarterly* 49 (1987) 1–13.

[15] For an indication of the 'classes' admitted, see W. A. Meeks, *The First Urban Christians: The Social World of the Apostle Paul* (New Haven: Yale University Press, 1983) pp. 51–73.

[16] On the situation that created the 'exclusiveness' of the community behind 1 John, see R. E. Brown, *The Epistles of John* (Anchor Bible 30; New York: Doubleday, 1982) pp. 47–115. On the Pauline communities, see Meeks, *First Urban Christians*, pp. 84–107.

[17] For the documentation, see J. Jeremias, *Jerusalem in the Time of Jesus: An Investigation into Economic and Social Conditions during the New Testament Period* (London: SCM Press, 1969) pp. 310–12.

[18] Jeremias, *Jerusalem*, p. 312.

material established as authentic by means of the criterion of dissimilarity.[19]

The value of this criterion obviously depends upon the balanced use of the criterion of dissimilarity. We are able to establish that there is an authentic record of Jesus' having shared his table with the people to whom Israel would have refused admittance. We are also able to point to different forms of reports of this activity of Jesus in the gospels. There are narrative records of Jesus' sharing his own table with sinners (for example, Mark 2:15; Luke 15:1–2). There are parables in which Jesus uses the gathering of the broken and the sinful from the highways and the byways as a symbol of the presence of the Kingdom of God (for example, Matt. 20:1–16, 21:28–32; Luke 14:12–24). They all 'cohere' with Jesus' extraordinary practice of table-fellowship with the broken people. Material from a variety of literary forms and different traditions forms a growing weight of evidence indicating one of the features of the public life of Jesus of Nazareth. Across all the gospels we find reports of the activity and the teaching of Jesus that is coherent with what appears to have been one of the marks of his lifestyle: table-fellowship with the broken people.

The final criterion, multiple attestation, has been described as follows:

> This is a proposal to accept as authentic material which is attested in all, or most, of the sources which can be discerned behind the synoptic Gospels.[20]

Although generally used to evaluate material that appears only in the Synoptic Gospels, in our case it can be extended. Scholars generally look to the various sources that were supposedly used by the Synoptic Gospels: Mark, 'Q', the material unique to Matthew and the material unique to Luke, testing whether the same aspect of the practice or teaching of Jesus is attested across these various sources.

The practice of Jesus' sharing his meals with the outcasts has been recorded across the various 'sources': e.g. Mark 2:15–16 (the *Marcan source*); Matt. 11:16–19 and Luke 7:31–35 (*the 'Q' source*); Matt. 20:1–16; 21:28–32 (*the Matthean source*); Luke 15:1–2; 19:1–10 (*the Lucan source*).[21] However, if our understanding of the eucharistic material that we have examined is correct, then the narratives

---

[19] Perrin, *Rediscovering*, p. 43.

[20] Perrin, *Rediscovering*, p. 45.

[21] Perrin, *Rediscovering*, pp. 102–8.

recorded there can also be added to the 'multiple attestations'. There, in a very special way, Jesus is 'sharing his table'.

While none of the eucharistic material examined comes from 'Q' or is unique to Matthew, the multiplication of the bread and the sharing of Jesus' table with sinners, betrayers and deniers on the night before he died can be found in Mark. It has been repeated, by Matthew and Luke, each in his own way. Luke, however, adds a further shared meal to this list in his account of the Emmaus journey. As well as the abundant attestation of this practice in Mark, 'Q', Matthew and Luke, Jesus also deliberately shares his table with his broken and sinful disciples in John 13:1–38. All the Gospel traditions witness to Jesus' sharing his table with the outcasts, the sinners and the broken.

This reflection upon how Jesus of Nazareth shared his table shows that we are in touch with one of the authentic practices of Jesus' public life. Such a practice was not invented by the early Church, which eventually tended to move in the opposite direction, seeing itself as 'over against' the sinful world. It came to the story-tellers and the missionaries who formed the Gospel traditions from the memory of Jesus' own lifestyle. This conclusion is admitted by all who have investigated the life and practice of the historical Jesus.[22]

> His table-fellowship with 'tax-collectors and sinners' . . . is not a proclamation in words at all, but an acted parable; it is the aspect of Jesus' ministry which must have been most meaningful to his followers and most offensive to his critics.[23]

The early Church founded its understanding of the Eucharist on the basis of the dangerous memory of Jesus' table-fellowship. We have traced the theme of the presence of Jesus to the broken in the eucharistic material used by all the Evangelists and by Paul. This has forced us to ask the question: where did this remarkably consistent theme come from? As the early Church 'remembered' its eucharistic

---

[22] See, for example, G. Bornkamm, *Jesus of Nazareth* (London: Hodder & Stoughton, 1963) pp. 80–1; C. H. Dodd, *The Founder of Christianity* (London: Collins, 1971) pp. 43–7, 75–9; Perrin, *Rediscovering*, pp. 102–8; B. F. Meyer, *The Aims of Jesus* (London: SCM Press, 1979) pp. 158–62; E. P. Sanders, *Jesus and Judaism* (Philadelphia: Fortress Press, 1985) pp. 174–211, 270–81; A. Nolan, *Jesus Before Christianity: The Gospel of Liberation* (London: Darton, Longman & Todd, 1977) pp. 37–42; G. Lohfink, *Jesus and Community: The Social Dimension of Christian Faith* (New York/Philadelphia: Paulist Press/Fortress Press, 1984) pp. 18–20, 42, 93; G. Theissen, *The Shadow of the Galilean: The Quest of the Historical Jesus in Narrative Form* (London: SCM Press, 1987) pp. 97–108. See the reflections of J. P. Mackey, *Jesus the Man and the Myth* (London: SCM Press, 1979) pp. 142–59.

[23] Perrin, *Rediscovering*, p. 102.

beginnings, it was also faced with the dangerous memory of Jesus' sharing his table with the broken people of his society and culture. The Eucharist was no exception to this practice. As Jesus shared his table with the broken and the outcasts, early Christians were being summoned to share their eucharistic table with the broken.

Although a developing liturgy and theology of Eucharist can be traced in the New Testament record of eucharistic celebrations, these records are founded on the bedrock of the memory of Jesus' meals throughout his ministry. It is not as a perfect Church welcoming a perfect people to its table that the earliest Christian communities understood the celebration of the Eucharist. Looking back to the experience of failure and sinfulness that had marked the historical beginnings of the Church, the New Testament authors spoke boldly of the love of Jesus, sharing his table, his body and his blood with them . . . and for them.

A Question to the Church

As I began these reflections, I mentioned the necessarily critical function that the Word of God must cultivate over against the tradition. Exercising this critical function is becoming increasingly more difficult in the contemporary Catholic Church.[24] This is one crucial area where we need to ask whether or not the theology and practice of the Church is at one with the Gospel message that we proclaim.

It is here that I believe we must go quietly forward, raising the critical question, asking the institution of the Church just why it was instituted in the first place. Pope John Paul II has written of this difficult task within a community:

> The attitude of solidarity does not contradict the attitude of opposition; opposition is not inconsistent with solidarity. The one who voices his opposition to the general or particular rules or regulations of the community does not thereby reject his membership; he does not withdraw his readiness to act and work for the common good . . . In order for opposition to be constructive, the structure, and beyond it the system of communities of a given society must be such as to allow the opposition that emerges from the soil of solidarity not only to *express* itself within the framework of the given community but also to *operate* for its benefit. The structure of a human community is correct only if it admits not just the presence of a justified opposition but also that practical effectiveness re-

---

[24] See the correspondence pages in the Melbourne Catholic weekly, the *Advocate*, 7, 14 and 21 July 1988. They represent the responses of many Catholics to a public lecture I gave, which outlined some of the conclusions of this study.

quired by the common good and the right of participation.[25]

An important feature of all forms of Christian life is the celebration of the Lord's Table. The Roman Catholic tradition sees the Eucharist as 'the source and summit of the Christian life' (*Lumen Gentium* 11; *Sacrosanctum Concilium* 10). At the heart of a Christian community is the call to the authentic celebration of Eucharist. But the Christian life is not limited to its *liturgical celebration* of the Eucharist. The celebration is the place where the whole 'rhythm' of the Christian life can be perceived (its source), and the ideal that challenges the Christian to love more (its summit). The celebration of the Eucharist also demands the living of eucharistic lives: 'They offer the divine victim to God *and themselves along with it*' (*Lumen Gentium* 11: my emphasis).

Our study has indicated that part of the message of the New Testament on the celebration of the Eucharist is a message of the Lord's presence to the broken. The New Testament texts on the Eucharist have been produced by a Christian people aware of their sinfulness, nourished and challenged at the eucharistic table.

The New Testament, however, also indicates that the earliest communities felt there were situations in which they had the right, and even the duty, to exclude certain members from the community and its life.[26] Particularly important in this regard are 1 Corinthians 5 and Hebrews 6:1–8.[27] There can be no selective reading of the New Testament to argue for a 'free for all' admission to the eucharistic table. This study must not be understood in that way. It is important to be aware that the early Church experienced a growing sense

---

[25] K. Wojtyla, *The Acting Person* (Analecta Husserliana X; Dordrecht: D. Reidel, 1979) pp. 286–7. Stress in original. The Pope is writing of the philosophical notion of human community, but his argument holds good for the 'common good' advocated and promoted by the Institution of the Church as a community.

[26] For a survey of the contemporary discussion of sociological processes behind this practice, see D. Tidball, *An Introduction to the Sociology of the New Testament* (Exeter: Paternoster Press, 1983) pp. 104–22.

[27] It is sometimes suggested that Matt. 5:23–24 (reconciling oneself with one's brother before offering sacrifice) is pertinent to this discussion. The text is not eucharistic. The passage may well be dominical, and presupposes the sacrificial system in Jerusalem, not the Christian Eucharist. See W. D. Davies & D. C. Allison, *The Gospel According to Saint Matthew*, (International Critical Commentary; Edinburgh: T. & T. Clark, 1988) vol. I, pp. 516–18; W. F. Albright & C. S. Mann, *Matthew* (Anchor Bible 26; New York: Doubleday, 1971) p. 62. Indeed, the message of Matt. 5:23–24 is further indication of the centrality of the case I have argued. As J. P. Meier, *The Vision of Matthew* (New York: Paulist Press, 1979) p. 245 remarks: 'In a sense, Jesus' basic teaching on the union of the love of God and love of neighbor is summed up in this parable. An alienated brother alienates us from God, no matter how splendid be the liturgy we perform.' See also E. Schweizer, *The Good News According to Matthew* (London: SPCK, 1978) p. 119.

of 'exclusiveness', which necessarily led to the eventual elimination
of certain people from the community, and thus from the Table of
the Lord. The exclusion from the community, as it is evidenced in
the New Testament, was primarily based in the early Church's
growing understanding of the person of Jesus and its response to
him as a community of believers.[28]

Even Paul's intervention in Corinth, demanding that the man in
an incestuous relationship 'be removed from among you' (1 Cor.
5:2) is motivated by the theme of the final coming of Christ, 'that his
spirit may be saved in the day of the Lord Jesus' (5:5). The need for
purity in the community is also founded upon a Christological
motivation:

> Cleanse out the old leaven that you may be a new lump,
> as you really are unleavened. For Christ, our paschal lamb, has
> been sacrificed. Let us, therefore, celebrate the festival, not
> with the old leaven, the leaven of malice and evil, but with the
> unleavened bread of sincerity and truth. (5:7–8).

As Murphy-O'Connor has commented: 'The presence within the
community of an attitude incompatible with Christ puts the freedom of all at risk because the protective barrier against the value
system of the "world" (= "Sin") has been weakened.'[29] It is because
of this that such a flagrant moral disorder cannot be tolerated.

A community that is based upon the self-sacrificing love of Jesus,
the paschal lamb (see also 11:23–25) must live in recognition of that
fact. What has happened in Corinth is totally unacceptable on these
grounds. The Corinthians' tolerance of this situation, rather than
showing the quality of their self-giving love in imitation of Christ
(5:7; 11:23–25), places them outside the quality of the love of the
pagans among whom they live: 'There is immorality among you,
and of a kind that is not found even among the pagans' (v. 1). The

---

[28] See also Matt. 18:8–9, 15–20; 2 Thess. 3:6–15 and 1 John 5:16–17. For a comprehensive exegetical study, see G. Forkman, *The Limits of Religious Community: Expulsion
from the Religious Community within the Qumran Sect, within Rabbinic Judaism, and within
Primitive Christianity* (Coniectanea Biblica New Testament Series 5; Lund: Gleerup,
1972) pp. 115–217. For some indications of the Christological process, which inevitably led to some form of 'exclusion' in early Christian communities, see J. D. G. Dunn,
*Unity and Diversity in the New Testament: An Inquiry into the Character of Earliest
Christianity* (London: SCM Press, 1977): see esp. pp. 262–3, 306–7, 378–9. The early
patristic tradition also based its admission to the Eucharist on the faith of the
participant. See, for example, *The Didache* IX:5, K. Lake (ed.), *The Apostolic Fathers*
(Loeb Classical Library; Cambridge (USA): Harvard University Press, 1912) vol. 1,
p. 323, and Tertullian, *De Praescriptione*, 41 (PL 2:68–69). Catechumens, non-baptised,
unbelievers and heretics are excluded. No mention is made of sinful believers. Matt.
7:6 (not casting pearls before swine) is used in both of these passages.

[29] Murphy-O'Connor, *1 Corinthians*, p. 43. See the whole treatment of Barrett, *First
Epistle*, pp. 120–30.

exclusion flows logically from Paul's deepest beliefs concerning the
saving event of Jesus Christ's death and resurrection.[30]

The difficult passage of Hebrews 6:1–8 also advocates that
certain people be separated from the community. Here the Christological basis for such a separation is quite obvious. The author first
exhorts the recipients of the tract to accept the duty that they have
to progress in their Christian faith and practice (vv. 1–3).[31] They are
to go farther than 'the elementary doctrines of Christ and go on to
maturity' (v. 1). The reader is made immediately aware that the
teachings of the faith (vv. 2–3) are concerned with 'the doctrines of
Christ' (v. 1). However, in this journey to a mature Christianity
Christians will encounter the perils of apostasy (vv. 4–8). There is a
very clear indication of the nature of the apostasy involved: 'They
crucify the Son of God on their own account and hold him up to
contempt' (v. 6).[32] The general meaning of this difficult passage is
that some Christians, who have enjoyed all the privileges of the
Christian life (vv. 4–5), can repeat the arrogance and unbelief of the
original crucifiers of Jesus. B. F. Westcott has suggested that:

> Perhaps there is the further thought in the image of
> crucifixion that Christ dwells in the believer. To fall away
> from the faith is therefore to slay him.[33]

Now, as then, there can be no admission to the common union
that the Eucharist creates between both Christ and the believer and
the celebrating faithful among themselves (see 1 Cor. 10:16–17) for
those who do not or will not accept Jesus as the Christ, the Son of
God (see Mark 1:1; Matt. 16:16; Luke 9:20; Romans 1:1–4).

Nevertheless, the deep Christian faith, the genuine holiness and
the search for God in the lives of many people whom we traditionally exclude from the Eucharist is well known. As far as the New
Testament evidence is concerned, it appears as if the reasons for

---

[30] Forkman, *The Limits of Religious Community*, concludes his detailed study of 1 Cor. 5
(pp. 139–51): 'The community has gone over from the sphere of death and flesh, the
old context, to the new context of life and the spirit. The consequences ought to be:
He who does not want to walk in the new context has by this himself chosen to stay
in the old' (p. 149).

[31] I say 'author', 'recipients' and 'tract' in deference to my erstwhile teacher, a world
authority on Hebrews, A. Vanhoye. He opened his lectures on Hebrews in 1972 with
the words: 'The Letter of St Paul to the Hebrews is not a letter, nor written by St Paul,
nor addressed to the Hebrews.'

[32] Forkman, *Limits*, p. 176: 'It is a question of open, intentional and voluntary apostasy.
There is no recommending of measures from the community's side.'

[33] B. F. Westcott, *The Epistle to the Hebrews: The Greek Text with Notes and Essays*
(London: Macmillan, 1889) p. 151. See his whole treatment on pp. 142–53.

exclusion from the community, and thus from the Eucharist, was based on doctrinal principles, rather than moral ones.[34] Of course, as both 1 Corinthians 5 and Hebrews 6:1–8 indicate, there are often important moral issues that arise from a faulty Christology (1 Cor. 5 and Heb. 6:1–8) or a faulty Ecclesiology (1 Cor. 5).

What are we to conclude from this evidence? Perhaps what is urgently required, if the biblical argument pursued in this study has any importance, is a new set of criteria concerning admission to the Eucharist. There must certainly not be a 'free for all' approach to this central mystery of the Christian life. Yet the frank recognition of the truth of the New Testament's precious insight, that the Eucharist is always a gift of the Lord to his failing community, must not be lost. Somehow, a balance must be kept between a realistic understanding of the Eucharist as a place where sinners gather to be both nourished and challenged by their Lord, but also as a sacred encounter, which must not be cheapened through the admission of those who would make a mockery of such a 'communion'.

Loyalty to our tradition demands that we examine this delicate balance carefully. We have seen the importance of the early Church's understanding of Jesus' presence to his own failing disciples, and their obligation to continue that 'presence' in the celebration of the Eucharist. We are also aware that those who deliberately and publicly break 'communion' (*koinônia*) have no place at the celebration of our eucharistic 'communion'.

We need to develop better criteria concerning admission to the Table of the Lord. I would suggest that the major criterion might be the quality of a person's 'communion' with the Church at many other levels. It is the 'communion' created by genuinely eucharistic lives that is sacramentalised in the Church's eucharistic celebrations. In more concrete terms, should we exclude those who recognise the imperfection and even the sinfulness of their lives, but have no other options? Indeed, is there not a Christ-like gift of self that one regularly finds in these situations? Many people are suffering deeply in the ambiguity of their situation, yet maintain their loyalty to Christianity and its values. Should we exclude those who commit themselves to a daily following of the crucified Christ, and who identify in so many ways with the poor and suffering in society? Indeed, many of those excluded from the Eucharist belong to the poor and suffering in society. The only choices in life available to

---

[34] Forkman, *Limits*, p. 217 concludes his comprehensive study of this question by claiming that neither Jesus nor the early Church saw the holiness of the community as the important issue. It was 'the individual's standpoint in face of the message about the kingdom of God'.

them are those that at present exclude them from the Lord's Table.[35]

There are, no doubt, many who exclude themselves from the eucharistic table by their rejection of the person of Jesus and the ways of Jesus. 'Those who could not eat with Jesus were those who rejected him, not those whom he rejected: his welcome was for all who would respond to him. He made no exceptions.'[36] Does our present legislation make this distinction clearly enough? It is obvious that many pastors have taken this decision into their own hands. It would be better for the whole of the 'body of the Lord' if the intuitions of the pastors were supported by the Church as a whole, responding to the questions that the Word of God poses to traditions that may have become distorted over the centuries.[37] But it is only the whole of the 'body of the Lord', guided by its leadership, that can make that response. The exegete must play his part in laying bare the message of the Word, but it is the whole body of the Church that must decide.

It is here, however, that major difficulties arise. Before we can fully understand and make vital the Gospel message of the Eucharist as God's saving action in the lives of the many broken people who look to him for just that, we must come to grips with the brokenness of our own Church and all its structures, and the deep brokenness of the lives of each one of us who make up that Church.

Indeed, the present difficulties in the Catholic Church over the proper exercising of a critical role — voicing 'opposition to the general or particular rules or regulations of the community' — are an indication of that particular institution's 'brokenness'. What is perhaps even more worrying is that these difficulties also indicate a deepening rift in the 'communion' needed for genuine eucharistic celebrations (see 1 Cor. 11:17–34). It is, as Paul has said, a question of correctly 'discerning the body of the Lord' (see 1 Cor. 11:29).

Is there not, in many of the attacks and counter-attacks of contemporary divisions within the Church, the real danger of deliberate pain and suffering being imposed on part of 'the body of the Lord'. Apart from the clearly intended injury that the various

---

[35] A powerful witness to this can be found in J. Feighery, 'Street People's Mass', *Tablet* 243 (1989) 347–8. For some further reflections, see W. F. Stolzman, 'Communion for Repenting Sinners?', *Clergy Review* 65 (1980) 322–7.

[36] P. Considine, 'Remarriage and the Eucharist', *Priest and People* 3 (1989) 226–7 (the whole article: pp. 226–9).

[37] Forkman, *Limits*, p. 216: 'There is a risk of present-day Christian communities drawing limits for the religious community in a way which is fundamentally alien to primitive Christianity.'

parties wish to inflict upon one another,[38] most of this discussion completely ignores the cries of the genuinely suffering and the poor. They are the ones who have no word in the theoretical discussions, but who ultimately bear the consequences of them.

Here we are at the heart of our problem. The Church as a whole must come to a deeper realisation that she described herself well at the Second Vatican Council: 'The Church, clasping sinners to her bosom, at once holy and always in need of purification, follows constantly the path of penance and renewal' (*Lumen Gentium* 8). This realisation must be reflected in all her traditions and structures.

While such an affirmation is relatively easy to state in principle, it is very difficult to put into practice. To render this teaching part of the day-to-day life of the Church would mean questioning traditions that have developed in an era when the Church's understanding of herself was more in terms of the perfect society, rather than a pilgrimage of sinners.

> The full power to be a witness to Christ, which is given to the church and to all its members, has been converted into the claim that the Church is the rich and gracious mediator of grace and salvation. Thus the church has become blind to its essential poverty (cf. 2 Cor. 4:8; Rev. 3:17). The glorious baroque church buildings, with their gilded altar walls and lovely angels in the blue skylike ceiling, clearly bear one message: a person who has entered the church has already entered the heavenly kingdom. Thus the church, with its sacraments, seems to have fallen victim to the temptation to represent, if not almost to replace, the glory of God's own kingdom.[39]

In concrete terms: does our present practice of Eucharist indicate a Church 'clasping sinners to her bosom'?[40]

Conclusion

As we proclaim the gospels we must come to realise more that it is not only to the failing and broken disciples of the Gospel stories

---

[38] For example, B. Payne, 'He is Risen', *Care Newsletter* (March 1989) 3, writes of an Australian Catholic theologian: 'Dr Coffey is strictly a parasitic form of life — he's strictly a retailer, passing on opinions he's picked up overseas.' He then attacks me through an appropriation of the words of Job: 'Here is one that must ever be clouding the truth of things with ill-considered words.'

[39] Barth, *Rediscovering*, p. 54.

[40] In a detailed note showing the similarities yet important differences between the meals celebrated at Qumran (see especially 1QS 6:2–6) and the early Christian meals, Léon-Dufour, *Sharing*, pp. 354–5, note 49, points out that, contrary to the Christian Eucharist, the 'unclean' were excluded at Qumran! Does this presuppose too much about the Christian practice of Eucharist?

themselves that Jesus comes in his eucharistic presence. He is present to the failing and broken disciples of all places and all times: his fragile yet grace-filled Church, in all its brokenness, 'at once holy, and always in need of purification' (*Lumen Gentium* 8).

However, it is easy to raise a questioning finger to the institution and feel that we have done our job. We are touching here a basic injustice of which we are all guilty. We have a tendency, in this matter, to preach one message and live another. To frequent the Eucharist full of my own self-righteousness and worthiness is to leave no space for the presence of a eucharistic Lord who seeks me out in my brokenness. He challenges me to go on taking the risky and difficult task of the Christian life, in imitation of him.

In 1548 the very first English Order of Communion carried a prayer entitled 'The Prayer of Humble Access' enshrining an understanding of the Eucharist that had come from the pen of Thomas Cranmer. It has been modified since the sixteenth Century.[41] It is still used as an optional prayer in both the First and Second Orders of the Holy Communion Services of the Church of England in Australia. Its present form is a challenge to all who are called to both celebrate and live the Eucharist:

> We do not presume
> to come to your table, merciful Lord,
> trusting in our own righteousness,
> but in your manifold and great mercies.
> We are not worthy
> so much as to gather up the crumbs under your table.
> But you are the same Lord
> whose nature is always to have mercy.
> Grant us, therefore, gracious Lord,
> so to eat the flesh of your dear Son Jesus Christ,
> and to drink his blood,
> that we may evermore dwell in him,
> and he in us.
>   Amen.[42]

---

[41] It became part of the *Book of Common Prayer* in 1662, and was used in that form until 1978. For a detailed commentary, see E. Daniel, *The Praise Book: Its History, Language and Contents* (Wells: Gardner Darton, 1948) 26th ed., pp. 375–6. I am indebted to Dean Graeme Lawrence of Newcastle Cathedral (Australia) for this reference.

[42] *An Australian Prayer Book for use together with The Book of Common Prayer, 1662* (Sydney: Anglican Information Office, 1978) p. 125.

A SELECT BIBLIOGRAPHY

The following bibliography lists only the major books and articles in English that, in various ways, have helped my study of the New Testament's eucharistic texts.

Barrett, C. K., *The First Epistle to the Corinthians* (Black's New Testament Commentaries; London: A. & C. Black, 1971).

Barth, M., *Rediscovering the Lord's Supper: Communion with Israel, with Christ, and Among the Guests* (Atlanta: John Knox Press, 1988).

Bornkamm, G., 'Lord's Supper and Church in Paul', in *Early Christian Experience* (London: SCM Press, 1969) pp. 123–60.

Bouyer, L., *Eucharist: Theology and Spirituality of the Eucharistic Prayer* (Notre Dame: University of Notre Dame Press, 1968).

Brown, R. E., *The Community of the Beloved Disciple: The Life, Loves and Hates of an Individual Church in New Testament Times* (London: Geoffrey Chapman, 1979).

Brown, R. E., 'Critical Biblical Exegesis and the Development of Doctrine', in *Biblical Exegesis and Church Doctrine* (New York: Paulist Press, 1985) pp. 26–53.

Considine, P., 'Remarriage and the Eucharist', *Priests and People* 3 (1989) 226–9.

Conzelmann, H., *1 Corinthians: A Commentary on the First Epistle to the Corinthians* (Hermeneia; Philadelphia: Fortress Press, 1975).

Cullmann, O., *Early Christian Worship* (Studies in Biblical Theology 10; London: SCM Press, 1953).

Dahl, N. A., 'Anamnesis: Memory and Commemoration in Early Christianity', in *Jesus in the Memory of the Early Church* (Minneapolis: Augsburg, 1976) pp. 11–29.

Dequeker, L., & Zuidema, W., 'The Eucharist and St Paul: 1 Cor. 11.17–34', *Concilium* 4 (1968) 26–31.

Dillon, R. J., *From Eye-Witnesses to Ministers of the Word: Tradition and Composition in Luke 24* (Analecta Biblica 82; Rome: Biblical Institute Press, 1978).

Donahue, J. R., *The Gospel in Parable* (Philadelphia: Fortress Press, 1988).

Dupont, J., 'The Meal at Emmaus', in J. Delorme *et al.*, *The Eucharist in the New Testament* (London: Geoffrey Chapman, 1965) pp. 105–21.

Fitzmyer, J. A., *The Gospel According to Luke* (Anchor Bible 28–28a; New York: Doubleday, 1981–85).

Forkman, G., *The Limits of Religious Community: Expulsion from the Religious Community within the Qumran Sect, within Rabbinic Judaism, and within Primitive Christianity* (Coniectanea Biblica New Testament Series 5; Lund: Gleerup, 1972).

Henrici, P., ' "Do this in remembrance of me": The sacrifice of Christ and the sacrifice of the faithful', *Communio: International Catholic Review* 12 (1985) 146–57.

Jeremias, J., *The Eucharistic Words of Jesus* (London: SCM Press, 1966).

Käsemann, E., 'The Pauline Doctrine of the Lord's Supper', in *Essays on New Testament Themes* (Studies in Biblical Theology 41; London: SCM Press, 1964) pp. 108–35.

Karris, R. J., 'God's Boundary-Breaking Mercy', *Bible Today* 24 (1986) 24–29.

Karris, R. J., *Luke: Artist and Theologian: Luke's Passion Account as Literature* (New York: Paulist Press, 1985).

Kingsbury, J. D., *Matthew as Story* (Philadelphia: Fortress Press, 1986).

Kodell, J., *The Eucharist in the New Testament* (Zacchaeus Studies: New Testament; Wilmington: Michael Glazier, 1989).

Laurance, J. D., 'The Eucharist as the Imitation of Christ', *Theological Studies* 47 (1986) 286–96.

Léon-Dufour, X., *Sharing the Eucharistic Bread: The Witness of the New Testament* (New York: Paulist Press, 1987).

Luz, U., 'The Disciples in the Gospel according to Matthew', in G. Stanton (ed.), *The Interpretation of Matthew* (Issues in Religion and Theology; London: SPCK, 1983) pp. 98–128.

Martelet, G., *The Risen Christ and the Eucharistic World* (London: Collins, 1976).

Minear, P. S., 'Some Glimpses of Luke's Sacramental Theology', *Worship* 44 (1970) 322–31.

Moloney, F. J., 'The Eucharist as the Presence of Jesus to the Broken', *Pacifica* 2 (1989) 151–74.

Moloney, F. J., 'John 6 and the Celebration of the Eucharist', *Downside Review* 93 (1975) 243–51.

Moloney, F. J., *The Living Voice of the Gospel: The Gospels Today* (Melbourne: Collins Dove, 1986).

Moloney, F. J., 'When is John Talking about Sacraments?', *Australian Biblical Review* 30 (1982) 10–33.

Moloney, F. J., 'Whither Catholic Biblical Studies?', *Australasian Catholic Record* 66 (1989) 83–93.

Murphy-O'Connor, J., *Becoming Human Together: The Pastoral Anthropology of St Paul* (Good News Studies 2; Wilmington: Michael Glazier, 1982).

Murphy-O'Connor, J., 'Eucharist and Community in First Corinthians', *Worship* 50 (1976) 370–85 and 51 (1977) 56–69.

Murphy-O'Connor, J., *1 Corinthians* (New Testament Message 10; Wilmington: Michael Glazier, 1979).

Neyrey, J., *The Passion According to Luke: A Redaction Study of Luke's Soteriology* (New York: Paulist Press, 1985).

O'Toole, R. F., *The Unity of Luke's Theology: An Analysis of Luke–Acts* (Good News Studies 9; Wilmington: Michael Glazier, 1984).

Perrin, N., *Rediscovering the Teaching of Jesus* (London: SCM Press, 1967).

Power, D. N., 'The Holy Spirit: Scripture, Tradition, and Interpretation', in G. Wainwright (ed.), *Keeping the Faith: Essays to Mark the Centenary of Lux Mundi* (London: SPCK, 1989) pp. 152–78.

Rensberger, D., *Johannine Faith and Liberating Community* (Philadelphia: Westminster Press, 1988).

Robbins, V. K., 'Last Meal: Preparation, Betrayal, and Absence', in W. Kelber (ed.), *The Passion in Mark: Studies on Mark 14–16* (Philadelphia: Fortress Press, 1976) pp. 21–40.

Senior, D., 'The Eucharist in Mark: Mission, Reconciliation, Hope', *Biblical Theology Bulletin* 12 (1982) 67–72.

Senior, D., *The Passion of Jesus in the Gospel of Mark* (Passion Series 2; Wilmington: Michael Glazier, 1984).

Senior, D., *The Passion of Jesus in the Gospel of Matthew* (Passion Series 1; Wilmington: Michael Glazier, 1985).

Senior, D., & Stuhmueller, C., *The Biblical Foundations for Mission* (New York: Orbis Books, 1983).

Stolzman, W. F., 'Communion for Repenting Sinners?', *Clergy Review* 65 (1980) 322–7.

Tannehill, R. C., *The Narrative Unity of Luke–Acts: A Literary Interpretation* (Foundation & Facets; Philadelphia: Fortress Press, 1986).

Theissen, G., 'Social Integration and Sacramental Activity: An Analysis of 1 Cor. 11:17–34', in *The Social Setting of Pauline Christianity: Essays on Corinth* (Philadelphia: Fortress Press, 1982) pp. 145–74.

Willis, W. L., *Idol Meat in Corinth: The Pauline Argument in 1 Corinthians 8 and 10* (SBL Dissertation Series 68; Chico: Scholars Press, 1985).

INDEX OF AUTHORS